CELTIC TRADITIONS

Druids, Faeries, and Wiccan Rituals

SIRONA KNIGHT

CITADEL PRESS
Kensington Publishing Corp.
www.kensingtonbooks.com

CITADEL PRESS books are published by

Kensington Publishing Corp.
850 Third Avenue
New York, NY 10022

All Kensington titles, imprints, and distributed lines are available at special quantity discounts for bulk purchases for sales promotions, premiums, fund raising, educational, or institutional use. Special book excerpts or customized printings can also be created to fit specific needs. For details, write or phone the office of the Kensington special sales manager: Kensington Publishing Corp., 850 Third Avenue, New York, NY 10022, attn: Special Sales Department, phone 1-800-221-2647.

Kensington and the K logo Reg. U.S. Pat. & TM Office
Citadel Press is a trademark of Kensington Publishing Corp.

First printing 2000

10 9 8 7 6 5 4

Printed in the United States of America

Library of Congress Cataloging-in-Publication Data

Knight, Sirona, 1955–
    Celtic traditions : shamans, Druids, faeries, and Wiccan
rituals / Sirona Knight.
      p. cm.
    Includes bibliographical references and index.
    ISBN 0-8065-2135-X
    1. Magic, Celtic. 2. Mythology, Celtic. I. Title.
BF1622.C45K56 1999
290′.16—dc21
                                       99–29546
                                           CIP

For Anu, the Mother of the Gods

And for my ancestral mentor, Sir Bartram Reveley, who is
interred in the chancel at Mitford Church in England.

"Here lyeth a generous and virteous knight. He was
descended from a race of worshipful antiquities, loved."

Contents

Acknowledgments

I would like to express my deep love and appreciation to Michael, my spiritual partner and husband, and to Skylor, our son, for their eternal love, light, and laughter. And a special thank you to my folks, Allan and Betty Wendt, for their encouragement and for helping me with this book. Sincere thanks and blessings to the gifted members of the Druid College of the Sun, for their inspiring efforts and belief in my work. Deep thanks to all of the Celtic Goddesses and Gods and the spirits of the Earth, Air, Fire, and Water for their friendship and love and for helping me write this book!

Also, I would like to especially thank Mike Lewis, my editor, for his friendship and continued faith in my writing. Thanks go, too, to Steven Schragis, my publisher, who provided continual support and enthusiasm for my endeavors. I would also very much like to acknowledge and thank each of you who are reading this book and getting in touch with your Celtic roots!

I would like to acknowledge and thank Lady Maireid Sullivan for her beautiful music and empowering friendship (and for singing in our living room!). Special thanks to Melissa Dragich. Loving thanks and many blessings to three great witches, Patricia Telesco, Dorothy Morrison, and A. J. Drew (don't call him warlock!). Bright blessings to Marion Weinstein, Starhawk, and

ix

Patricia Monaghan, and special thanks to John Nelson for his friendship and for listening and actually understanding me.

Many thanks to everyone at *New Age Retailer* magazine, particularly Molly Trimble, for her faith in my work and her continued optimism. And thank you to everyone at *Magical Blend* magazine, especially the publisher, Michael Langevin, for his support. Blessings and thanks to Dan Liss at *Aquarius* magazine, to Rob McConnell at the X-Zone, and to MoonRaven and DragonHawk at Whispered Prayers.

I would also like to respectfully acknowledge and thank R. J. Stewart, Jean Markale, Peter Ellis, Janet and Colin Bord, Philip Carr-Gomm, Robin Williamson, Aine Minogue, Donovan, Alan Stivell, Loreena McKinnett, Steve McDonald, Medwyn Goodall, Derek Bell, Kim Robertson, and the many talented and creative authors, musicians, and artists who have kept Celtic Traditions and the spiritual message of the Celts alive and thriving!

Blessed Be! Blessed Be the Gods!
Sirona Knight
Beltane, 1999

INTRODUCTION

When I was sixteen, I went on a vacation to Scotland. As I walked through the gates of Edinburgh Castle, I saw my reflection in a nearby shop window, and for a few moments I didn't recognize myself. It was as if I had walked through a gateway to another time and place, yet it was as real as walking out my back door. I experienced an awakening, becoming aware of something inside myself I wasn't aware of before. It was as though I saw a reflection of my true nature. This otherworldly experience changed me permanently and spurred me to actively seek out my Celtic roots.

What I discovered on my quest, besides a few skeletons in the closet, was a roughly bound, inches-thick volume of family history, listing among other things, one of my Celtic ancestors from Northumberland as Sir Bartram Reveley, who is interred in the chancel at Mitford Church. His epitaph reads, "Here lyeth a generous and virteous knight. He was descended from a race of worshipful antiquities, loved." A handful of knights, a cavalier, a governor, a couple of infamous authors, and even James Smithson, who founded the Smithsonian Institute, all were listed in the family genealogy book. Such getting in touch with my Celtic roots led me further down the Druid path, resulting in my finally writing about Celtic spirituality and magic.

Whether by ancestry or evolution, recent surveys report that over 40 percent of people in the United States have Celtic roots. These figures are particularly significant when you realize most of the people living in this geographical locale reside in places that are not an extension of their ancestral history, which often leaves people with a feeling of rootlessness and disconnectedness. In this light, a large section of the population feels the urgent need to reconnect, identify, discover their origins, and integrate who they are in the twenty-first century. This need is being expressed in the current Celtic resurgence, which continues to gain momentum, not only in the United States, but throughout the world. One of the reasons is because Celtic spirituality is something universal, everything weaving together with no lines or separation between spirit and matter, time and space, or people and things.

Ancient traditions are not dead but only asleep, comfortably resting in world mythologies. Myth is a wellspring of creativity and much more efficient than history because it conveys not only the facts of events and experience, but also the emotions and spirit of the story. Studying myth, legend, and folklore becomes a way to awaken the ancient traditions. It is our challenge to positively adapt them to our times, modern concerns, and contemporary society.

Today, many people are coming around to realizing the deep connection we have with nature, something the Druids knew long ago. Still more of us are coming around on a global level. Whether it reflects each of us acting out or discovering something in our genetic coding and/or a global movement toward attaining a more evolved, cyclic, and connected way of thinking, the recent Celtic resurgence has inspired many people to rediscover their Celtic roots.

Many people are beginning to hear the call of the Goddess, connecting with the sacred spirit of the land. Throughout history, humankind has collectively rejected and polluted the sacred Earth, embracing the ethics of depletion rather than renewal. If we want to remain as a species on this planet much longer, we must now heal our Mother, communicate with her once again, and understand her needs and desires much as we do our own. One profound way to do this is by connecting with the energies and wisdom of the Goddess and God, and thus with the sacred spirit that sleeps within the land.

To awaken the sleepers is to awaken in ourselves the potential powers and abilities that are dormant. Celtic myth, folklore, poetry, and music are like time capsules, set in place for an era when the sleepers awaken en masse. This knowledge and the keys of the magical traditions smolder within the arts and crafts of the people, flickering like an eternal flame. For example, when you hear traditional Celtic songs, with harp, fiddle, whistle, and drum, something in you stirs, something that was sleeping but has now awakened, arising within you. The most distinguishing quality of Celtic traditions is this hint of enchantment and mystery.

Humanity and the land are inseparable aspects of our planet. Living traditions such as Druidism and the Faery tradition show us how to enter the boundless realms of inspiration, creativity, and spirit. We are the ancestors to future generations. Joining together, we can create a difference in the world now and in the future for thousands of years to come.

It is a time to begin the great quest, a time of personal sovereignty and self-realization, which are both expressions of individual freedom that do not conform to the status quo. The world is thankfully coming to a more circular, feminine way of thinking, whereas before it had been linear and unevenly masculine. This corresponds to the Celtic world, where everything has a circular, and less linear, slant to it, and where women and men are equals.

This book provides a broad background in ancient Celtic traditions, tying many sources together into one. At the end of each chapter, except the last, I have purposely included an experiential visualization. The last chapter concludes with a hands-on Druid healing ritual for the Earth. My intention in writing this book was to combine left-brain information with right-brain visualizations in an effort to create a balance from which to navigate—both in this world and the Otherworld. I respectfully hope that the information provided within the following pages is useful and valuable as you embark or continue upon the great adventure.

CELTIC
TRADITIONS

1

CELTIC ROOTS
AND SHAMANISM

One night at twilight,
walking between worlds
the ancestors speak
in ancient tongues,
melodic voices
shapes arise and sway
memories carry you away.

From "The Ancestors Come Alive,"
by Sirona Knight

The journey of the Celts began thousands of years ago, at a
time when people were drastically altering their lifestyles;
even once-nomadic hunters started to settle down and grow
their food. From these beginnings, the Celts moved across
Europe, trading goods and ideas with a variety of cultures
whom the Celts influenced and who influenced the Celts.
Because the Celtic people were actually a collection of tribes,
each with its own separate leader, the heritage of the Celts is as

varied as the people themselves—from the Irish to the Scottish and from the Welsh to the Gaelic.

Celtic roots represent the essential source from which the later Celtic spiritual traditions originate, and accordingly, these roots contain concepts universal throughout the scope of Celtic spirituality. This commonality revolves around the idea of the "Mother Goddess," who comprises the whole of the universe; all the other Goddesses and Gods depict aspects of the Mother Goddess. The Mother Goddess of the Celts was Danu, whose name means "divine water." The Danube River takes its name from her, and it may very well be that the Celtic civilization evolved at the headwaters of the Danube. A second common concept among Celtic traditions is their spiritual connection with the land. This stems from the first concept because the Mother Goddess and the land (Earth) are One to the Celts.

This connection to nature related to every aspect of the social structure and shamanic practices of the Celts. From the seed in the soil sprouts the tree, which moves upward toward the light. The roots residing in the soil symbolize the connection to the seed, whereas the stock or trunk moving upward branches out and creates a weave of life. Rivers that spring from the source move on a course that leads to the infinite ocean of Oneness. The Celts embraced this simple beauty with a very accurate understanding of nature and, in turn, the metaphysical universe around them.

From Hunters to Planters

An agrarian people, the Celts finely tuned themselves in to the natural cycles of the Earth. As a result, their spiritual traditions were in harmony with these cycles. The eight Celtic festival days exemplify this, in that each day's ritual acts out the role of Mother Nature or the Goddess as she moves through the various seasons; from Yule (the winter solstice), when the cycle of light begins again, to Hertha's Day (the beginning of spring), when seeds are planted, to the summer solstice and on to Hellith's Day (the autumnal equinox), when thanks are given for the harvest. Each of these seasonal festivals connects the participants to the Earth, which is an embodiment of the Goddess. The rituals express the Celtic people's reverence to the great Goddess, who affects every aspect of their agrarian way of life.

An interesting thing happens to people's perception of the world when they move from being hunters and gatherers to being planters and herders. For one thing, they suddenly know where their next meal is coming from. Also, to someone who hunts and gathers his or her food, the world is one of predator versus prey in which survival depends on either killing or being killed. Even gathering is competitive because people are in competition with other species of animals for food that grows wild. To hunters, the idea of a natural organic end to life is foreign because in their world, death is usually a result of violence. In such a system, people tended to view their world in terms of linear events rather than as a circular pattern.

Seeing the world in terms of events instead of patterns has a profound effect on people's spiritual view of the world around them. Hunters believed in magic, but their magic was very event driven and was often a means of explaining their experiences in life. Magic to the Celts and other early agrarian societies consisted of working with and influencing the natural and organic patterns, which were part of their everyday lives and of every living thing. Essentially, hunters work immediate magic so that they will be successful in a specific upcoming hunt, whereas planters use long-term magic to ensure that the whole pattern or cycle is successful and continues to be fruitful for generations to come.

When people move from being nomadic hunters and gatherers toward agriculture and the domestication of animals, they go from a relationship with the universe based on killing or being killed, to one of aligning themselves with the cycle of the seasons and the art of planting, harvesting, and collecting the seeds for the next planting. Suddenly, life takes on a much more circular flow. Death, instead of being a result of violence, becomes a natural phase of life and part of the natural cycle of rebirth, life, and death. In all Celtic traditions, the triune or threefold concept recurs and is an elemental part of the Celts' perception of the universe.

Another important difference between hunters and planters is how they view the spirits of their ancestors. The hunters fear the ghosts of their ancestors, which they perceive in physical terms. They frequently believe the spirits of their ancestors should be avoided because they mean the hunters harm. In contrast, the planters revere and work with the energy of their ancestors, which they perceive in a more mystical, metaphysical light. For example, the Celts often deified their ancestors, and each generation added to the mythology of previous generations. (The Tuatha De Danann were all descended from the one common ancestor, Anu or D'Anu, who later became the Great Mother of the Celts, and her offspring were the Celtic pantheon of Gods and Goddesses.) In this way, the Celtic festivals and rituals took on a deeper meaning, connecting the individual to the whole group and in turn the whole of the universe.

Joseph Campbell, in his book *Primitive Mythology: The Masks of God,* describes the difference between hunters and planters in these terms:

> When the rites and mythologies even of the most primitive planting villages are compared with those of any tribe of hunters, it is readily seen that they represent a significant deepening both of religious feeling and of the commitment of the individual to communal life; the hunters, comparatively, are rugged individualists. For it is in the rituals and mysteries of the group that the planters not only achieve their sense of the entity of the sib (blood relations), but also learn the way

by which the dangers of the journey to the happy land of the dead are to be overcome and the company joined of the ancestors, who from there work as a continuing presence in the living memory of the rite.

Once planters began to see their world as a continuous cycle driven by natural recurrent forces, they also understood the totality of how these forces came together as One. Campbell described this transition of the perception of the planters with the suggestion that:

> The first plantings should be sought, according to this conjecture, in that broad equatorial where the vegetable world has supplied not only the food, clothing, and shelter of man since time out of mind, but also his model of the wonder of life—in its cycle of growth and decay, blossom and seed, wherein death and life appear as transformation of a single, superordinated, indestructible force.

This single, superordinated, indestructible force transforming the perception and world of the planters manifested itself in the form of the Goddess, who is synonymous with the Earth because both are sources of creation. The Celts in particular saw the seasons and the changes of life as part of the many faces of the Goddess, whatever her name. The emergence of the Mother Goddess transformed the peoples of Europe, greatly influencing the Celts and other early planter societies such as those that sprang up around the Mediterranean Sea.

The Emergence of the Mother Goddess

Reverence toward the Earth, particularly in the image of the Earth Mother, is widespread throughout the world. Originating in the magical nature of planting and growth, and the ceremonial approach to the seeding, growing, and harvesting of plants, this concept relies heavily on a practical working knowledge of the cycles of the Earth, in addition to a spiritual connection with these natural patterns. The seeds are planted within the land, and they in turn come to life and grow to produce flowers and food. After the food is harvested, the plants return to seed and their remains are composted back into the soil, providing fodder for future generations.

To early planter societies the Mother Goddess symbolized fertility, sexual union, and the entire complex of birth, growth, and death of plants, animals, and people. The Mother Goddess is found in divine pantheons throughout the world, sometimes limited and sometimes all-encompassing, in such a way as to be the sole deity. Often the Mother Goddess is a chthonic earth deity, who is the source of all things living and growing. Some of the most sacred symbols of Paleolithic and Neolithic humanity were symbols of the womb, the source of life and fountainhead of all creativity.

Numerous Goddess figures dating back to 10,000 B.C. have been found around the areas of eastern Spain, across North Africa to the Nile, and in the Jordan, Mesopotamia, India, and Ceylon. It is significant that before this date, there are no Goddess artifacts and for the most part no pictures of women. Many of the objects found are crudely carved out of stone but are definite representations of the female shape, often in the pregnant form, relating back to the female power of creation. The year 10,000 B.C. coincides with the beginnings of the civilizations along the Mediterranean.

The Great Mother of the Mediterranean region is Cybele, who influenced the concept of other Mother Goddesses in the area, such as Inanna, Ishtar, and Aphrodite. These Goddesses greatly resemble one other. As the Great Mother she was the source of life, identified with nature and the Earth. In addition, Cybele was the Great Mother of Phrygia, as well as being the Anatolian name of the ancient Mediterranean Goddess of nature, and also Goddess of the mountains, forests, and Earth, and of reproduction. The Greeks identified her with Rhea, wife of Cronus and Mother of Zeus.

This last tie interestingly enough leads us back into the roots of Celtic spirituality, in that Albion, the ancient name for Britain, derives from the mythology of the Titans. The Titans are the Sky-Gods and Earth Goddesses, whose origins are derived from the beginnings of humankind. This shows that the Celtic traditions are linked to the emergence of the Goddess within human perception, and because of this tie, their traditions are some of the oldest existing in the world today.

Regarding the concept of the Mother Goddess and how it relates to the Celts, Jean Markale, author and authority on Celtic studies, in the book *Women of the Celts* writes, "The most likely incarnation of the Indo-European Mother-Goddess concept is a deity continually mentioned by both [the] Welsh and Irish although she is never the heroine of any story and appears only to give her children a name. This figure is the Welsh Don, the Irish Dana or Ana." Don, also called Danu, is the sister of Math and the mother of the master shape-shifter God Gwydion. She is the fountainhead of a line of Gods, Goddesses, heroines, and heroes, and considered the Great Mother of the race of the Tuatha de Danann, or people of the Goddess Dana, and is mentioned in all the Irish legends.

Once these pre-Celtic peoples settled down and became planters, Dana was the name they gave to this force of nature. As people became tied to the land, they began to build settlements and later city-states, such as those of Sumer and Egypt.

The Celtic Connection to the Mediterranean Cultures

In 300 B.C., the historian Hecataeus of Abdera wrote about an island inhabited by a people he called the Hyperboreans. These people had erected a magnificent sacred precinct of Apollo and a temple that was spherical in shape. The word *Boreas* in Greek means from where the North Wind comes, signifying the Hyperboreans as being a culture from the distant north. Ancient language scholar Zecharia Sitchin, in his book *When Time Began,* discusses these mysterious people. He writes:

> The legends regarding the Hyperboreans were thus mingled with the myths concerning Apollo and his twin sister, the Goddess Artemis. As the ancients told it, the twins were the children of the great God Zeus and their Mother Leto, a Titaness. Impregnated by Zeus, Leto wandered over the face of the Earth seeking a place to give birth to her children in peace, away from the wrath of Hera, the official wife of Zeus; Apollo was thus associated with the distant north. The Greeks and the Romans considered him a God of divination and prophecy; he circled the zodiac in his chariot.

Once again, this connection to the Titans recurs. Their relevance to the Celts comes in two forms: first, the Titans were the Sky-Gods, who preceded the classical Greek pantheon and thus harken back to a more ancient and earlier tradition. Second, the ancient name of Britain is Albion, who was one of the Titans, and all of those within Britain's shores are called the "children of Albion."

Apollo, the Greek sun God, rides on his chariot through the seasons and the signs of the Zodiac, which were very important to the Celts. The reference to a northern spherical temple that charts the course of the sun is an allusion to one of the greatest and most ancient sites in northern Europe, Stonehenge.

Archaeologists digging in the area around Stonehenge found bronze daggers, axes and maces, golden ornaments, decorated pottery, and polished stones. These discoveries, plus the smoothly dressed and carefully shaped stones at Stonehenge, initially led archaeologists to surmise that there existed a connection between the site and Minoan Crete and Mycenaean Greece. Located on the southwestern part of the Grecian mainland, Mycenae flourished in the sixteenth century B.C. Treasures excavated from the tombs of Mycenean kings showed the influence of foreign contacts, which included trading with Britain. In her book, *Dawn of the Gods,* Jacquetta Hawkes advances the idea that:

> At the time when Mycenaean kings were rising to a new wealth and power, a rather similar advance, although on a smaller scale, was taking place in southern England. There too a warrior aristocracy was ruling over peasants and herders and beginning to trade and to prosper and to be buried with appropriate extravagance. Among the possessions thus buried were a few objects that prove these chieftains to have had contacts with the Mycenaean world.

In addition to the Grecian artifacts found in the area around Stonehenge, other objects had a definite Egyptian influence. In particular, archaeologists found decorated beads and amber disks bound with gold, a craft method developed in Egypt. The evidence of so many artifacts indicates that the Celts extensively traded with both the Greeks and the Egyptians, most likely through the Phoenicians, who were renowned in the ancient world for being expert sailors. The Phoenicians set up a trading network that connected the Mediterranean cultures with other flourishing civilizations of the time, such as the Celts. The idea of goods being traded opens up the probability that ideas were also exchanged between these cultures, which accounts for the widespread appeal of the "Mother Goddess" concept, at least early on. These trading networks were an ancient web reminiscent of today's Internet (just a great deal slower). It was a way of linking goods, ideas, and people together.

This connection between Celtic culture and the cultures of the Mediterranean, including Egypt, Minoan Crete, and

Greece, reveals the flow of goods and ideas between the various cultures. These Mediterranean cultures are thought—because of the extensive historical record of their development—to be some of the more advanced cultures of their time.

Although less has been written about the Celts, their culture and traditions reached just as high a level of development as their Mediterranean counterparts. Out of necessity for their survival in the face of successive invasions, Celtic esoteric traditions remained oral, passed on by the Bards. Some of these oral traditions have only recently come to the forefront because they are finally being translated, written down, and published. For many centuries the Druids and Bards wisely kept the oral tradition of Celts alive, passing it from generation to generation. When the Celtic libraries were burned to the ground, unlike the destruction of the library at Alexandria, all of their ancient knowledge was not lost because the Celtic traditions continued orally and still thrive today.

The investigation into the people who built Stonehenge does not stop at this point but moves to an earlier civilization that influenced everyone who followed, from the Babylonians and Egyptians to the Celts and Greeks. The beginnings of Stonehenge were built between 2900 to 2600 B.C., a thousand years before extensive trading with Mediterranean sailors began. In addition, scholars such as Zecharia Sitchin, in the book *When Time Began,* have called Stonehenge a ". . . sanctuary constructed from colossal yet carefully-shaped blocks that make the cyclopean masonry of Mycenae look like children's bricks, and has nothing to compare with it in all prehistoric Europe."

Essentially a "temple to the sun," Stonehenge has been documented to be an ancient stellar observatory that tracked the movement of the sun and moon with calculated precision. Constructed in stages, with each stage drawing and improving upon its predecessor, Stonehenge, because of its age, was influenced by the traditions of ancient Egypt and Sumer. In the third millennium B.C., when Stonehenge was conceived, Egypt had been evolving its sanctuary along the Nile for centuries. The Sumerians, with their cities, writing, and scientific discoveries, had already existed for over a thousand years.

A connecting element in the whole puzzle is that the circle, a shape that is the most outstanding feature of Stonehenge, is essential to astronomical observations. In particular, the zodiac, or cycle of twelve constellations moving across the sky in the orbital plane of the planets, provides the root for this circular pattern. The Celts, Greeks, Egyptians, and Babylonians all used the zodiac, but its roots date back to the Sumerians.

With regards to the connection between the Sumerians and the zodiac, a most interesting discovery resulted from using modern technologies to find ancient sites. In this case, aerial observation revealed the existence of a vast and complex pattern of figures in the contours and landmarks around the area of Glastonbury, England. This pattern of figures forms a huge land chart of the zodiac. The Cymry of Wales gleaned their knowledge of the stars from the East, somewhere in Asia Minor, and laid out this pattern for the zodiac, which in Welsh is called *caer sidi*. Regarding the Sumerian connection, Dr. L. A. Waddell, in his book *Makers Of Civilization,* writes, "Detailed proofs are given in my former works for the Sumerian origin of the Cymry with approximate dates for the Sumerian colonizing occupation of parts of the British Isles by several immigrations from the Sargonic period of about 2700 B.C. onwards."

Sumer, most likely the first civilization in recorded time, was a collection of city-states around the lower Tigris and Euphrates rivers in what is now southern Iraq. Beginning as a collection of farming villages in 5000 B.C., Sumer rose to prominence and developed a collection of city-states, which began recorded history, in the sense that they developed a means of writing things down in a wedge-shaped writing style known as cuneiform. They were also one of the earliest recorded societies to have a spiritual tradition based on the Goddess, who in their case was Inanna. The Tigris and Euphrates Rivers have the reputation for being the birthplace of modern civilization. There is certainly some indication that the roots of Celtic traditions, which were linked to and formed at the same time as those of Egypt and Sumer, have evolved for over five thousand years.

The roots of Celtic traditions reach into the earliest beginnings of modern civilization, when people first began to collect and plant seeds. This resulted in their new awareness of the cycles of nature, which involved the elements of birth, death, and rebirth. The Celts watched the sun, moon, and stars as they moved through the heavens, affecting people's daily lives. The Earth Mother provided their food and way of life. Being in tune with her energy was essential to their survival. Humankind's connection to the Earth and relationship with the Mother Goddess was pure and uninhibited because people's existence depended on it. This occurred not only on a physical level, but also on a mental and spiritual one. The Celtic Druids became masters of magic because they were so in tune with everything around them, in a realm that moved beyond the physical into the mystical. Essentially, magic is a matter of energy, patterning, and timing. The effectiveness of the magic is a result of how well the pattern is put together, how much energy you put into it, and how well timed it is.

The Migration of the Celts to the British Isles

Pre-Celtic peoples built the megalithic monuments that dot the countryside all over northern and western Europe. Historians propose that these pre-Celtic peoples were the first peoples led by Druids, worshiping the sun at such sites as Stonehenge. These original Druids practiced an ancient Indo-European tradition that closely resembled that of the Brahmins in India and the Cult of the Dead of the Mediterranean. As the Celts migrated into the British Isles, they adopted and continued the Druidic tradition, while at same time bringing in and merging other ideas from places along the Mediterranean.

Unfortunately, no ancient texts exist on the subject and no one knows where the Celts began their journey to what eventually became their homes in England, Ireland, Scotland, Wales, Gael, and the coast of Brittany. The Celts were never a very unified nation but rather a collection of unstable tribes, known for their trading and artistic abilities. Because there was no single Celtic race, the Celts were primarily a conglomeration of different cultures or traditions coming together under the same banner, with their origins dating around 800 B.C. Indigenous peoples were first enslaved and then they merged together, with their common characteristics being language, basic locality, and overlapping spiritual traditions. An example of this cultural assimilation was when the Gaels entered Ireland and forced the Tuatha De Danann, who were the ancient inhabitants of Ireland, to give way. The Tuatha became the Gods and Goddesses of Celtic imagination and deities of the subterranean world.

Because of the weather changes and geographical upheavals that occurred toward the end of the Bronze Age, the Celts left their homeland in the Harz Mountains in central Germany, and from there they spread through northern and western Germany, as well as along the Baltic and North Sea coasts. Before long, they established trade relations with their neighbors around the Elbe and in the British Isles, particularly in Ireland, which was the beginning of one of the first Celtic migrations of Gaels into Ireland.

Due to climate changes at the end of the Bronze Age (530 B.C.), Western Europe suddenly became cold and wet again. As a result, the North Sea and Baltic coastlines became soggy marshland, which made this area uninhabitable for the Celts who had been living there. Archaeological evidence indicates that during this period, vast numbers of people migrated out of the area as a means of escaping the flooded regions. This exodus was one of the most important migrations of Britons to Great Britain. Not all of the Celts living by the Baltic and North Seas made for Britain; some journeyed to the Rhineland and from there to what later became Gaul, which is present-day France. Whenever the historians of antiquity mention the Gauls, there is always a reference to magical legends. The Gauls were regarded as an exceptional race, gifted with superhuman powers.

Irish history provides an excellent example of how people from many cultures migrated into the British Isles. The successive waves of invaders included the Cesair who came from Egypt, the Partholon who came from Greece, the Nemed who were descendants of the Nemed from Syria, the Fir Bolg who also came from Greece, and the Sons of Mil who came via Scythia, Egypt, and Spain.

In his book *The Druids,* author Peter Ellis discusses the invaders of Britain: "The first invader was Cesair, daughter of Bith who was son of Noah of the Hebrew myth. Bith was denied a place in the Ark and so Cesair advised him to build an idol with his companions Fintan and Ladra. The idol then told them to build a ship as Noah had done and take refuge in it. . . . After seven years they came to the shores of Ireland." In this story, Fintan is the only one to survive the deluge by turning himself into a salmon.

Both the Partholon and the Nemed are descendants of Magog, who was the son of Japhet, who was one of the three sons of Noah. Interestingly, modern Druid groups still honor Magog and Gog during ritual toasting. When the Partholon and Nemed invaded, they found the fierce Fomorii, the dark and sinister undersea dwellers of Irish myths. The plague killed Partholon and his followers. The Nemed were enslaved by the Formorians and paid a yearly tribute of two-thirds of their children and cattle. The Nemeds finally conquered the Formorians, killing Conann, the Formorian king, but the Nemed were so diminished they left Ireland.

The group of invaders called the Fir Bolg (Men of the Bags) were Nemedian survivors who returned to Ireland. They came from Greece where they had been enslaved and made to carry earth in bags. According to ancient tradition, the Fir Bolg were the first inhabitants of Ireland and were giants. They had no problem overcoming the Formorians and held Ireland after the death of the Nemed, until they were defeated by the Tuatha De Danann. The Fir Bolg then fled to the Aran Islands. The powerful rule of the Formorians was finally overcome by the Tuatha De Danann. The Milesians (Sons of Miled) were ancestors of the Gaels. They held the land after the Tuatha De Danann.

Each of these cultures brought its own ideas and also assimilated the ideas of the indigenous people, some of whom were the original Druids. Because these many waves of cultures migrating into Ireland came from a variety of places around the world, including the Mediterranean and Ireland, Irish culture became a melting pot of ideas that were prominent at the time, such as the concept of the "Mother Goddess." The migrating Celts brought with them their agrarian way of life and spiritual traditions that connected them to the land of their new-found homes in the British Isles.

Celtic Clans and Tribes

As the Celts settled in the British Isles, ancestral lineage and a connection to the land became even more of an integral part of their spiritual tradition. To the Celts, ancestors were divine energies inhabiting the land, which again was thought to be One with the Goddess. The importance of ancestral lineage is revealed in the social structure of the Celts, whose basic unit was the clan, which was like a large extended family. Beyond

the clan was the Celtic tribe, a conglomeration of clans united
by a common political and spiritual tradition. Both the clan and
the tribe were tied together by ancestry and a connection to a
particular locality. Generation after generation, as more of the
clan's ancestors were buried in a specific area, the clan's connection to that land reached beyond the physical into the spiritual, magical, and universal.

Anyone familiar with Scotland knows about the clans, such as
the MacGregors and MacDonalds, that still exist today. The
Scottish Clans mirror the clan system of the ancient Celts. In
turn, the Celtic clan system was reminiscent of the early Gaelic
family, eventually finding some of its roots in the ancient Indo-
European "gens." Common in Roman and Greek society, gens
were family units that drew their lineage from the male family
members. Unlike the gens, Celtic clans were matrilineal. Matrilineal descent is pre-Indo-European and, for the Celts, has its
origins in the Tuatha De Danann.

Ancient Britons counted all relatives as far as the ninth
removed. The ancient Gaels called this family unit the *fine*. This
stems from the same root as *Gwynedd,* which comes from
northwest Wales and the Veneti (and in turn is the name of the
Gallic people who inhabited the county around Vannes and
"Gwened" in Breton). In Ireland, when a family or clan reached
a certain size, it took the name of Deirbhfine, consisting of four
generations, from the father, called the *cenn-fine,* head or chief
of a family, and extending to the great-grandchildren. Outside
these four generations, the family would be divided into various
different branches, all entitled to a share of the inheritance
under the law of *gavelkind,* a characteristic of Irish, British, and
Breton societies that appears to be related to early German and
Celtic law.

Several clans or *fines* made up a tribe, which the Celts called
a *tuatha*. The basic political unit in Ireland, each *tuatha* (family)
was self-sufficient in that it possessed a well-defined social hier-

archy, from the chief or king down to the slave, with goods owned in common, its own rules and regulations, and its own Gods. The quasi-autocracy of a *tuatha* had quite a remarkable impact on the history of Celts and lies at the root of why the Celtic tribes were never able to unify politically, because the people's loyalty was traditionally to their *tuatha* and not to any Celtic nation as a whole.

The *tuatha,* or tribe, traces its roots back to totemism. Examples in Celtic mythology include King Conchobar of Ulster, chief of the Red Branch, and Finn, chief of the Fenians, who were both clan-like organizations subject to strict laws. In the case of the Tuatha De Danann, they were all descended from the one ancestor, the Goddess Dana. Each *tuatha* was autonomous. This led to a tendency toward anarchy. Each *tuatha* also had spiritual autonomy, in the sense that each Celtic tribe often worshiped its own Mother Goddess.

Politically separate, each *tuatha* had its own king, queen, leader, or chief. The concept of one all-ruling sovereign or king was a concept difficult for any self-respecting Celt to accept. The myth of the high king did produce attempts to unify society. The Gaels felt that they could only survive with a single authority, but that this authority would have to be both incontestable and flexible.

In *Women of the Celts,* Jean Markale writes:

Celtic Society was full of archaisms largely gathered and integrated from the original inhabitants of Western Europe. It was halfway between the patriarchal type of society, which was agricultural and based on the ownership of land by the father of the family, and matriarchal societies, in which the Mother, or women in general, remained the basic link in the family and a symbol of fertility.

Matriarchal order and lineages stem from the early concept that creation comes from women. Creation is a divine seed, stemming from the Mother. Plainly, the mother's identity is always certain while the father's is not. The man's role is to nurture and protect this seed. Unlike many paternal societies, the Celts treated women as equals. For example, when a woman came into a relationship with a man and she owned most of the wealth, she retained the decision-making power in regards to her wealth. This equality and coming together of the sexes is essentially what Celtic spiritual traditions are all about. Within the union of the female and male energies comes the concept of ancestry and the evolution of Celtic traditions.

Celtic Shamanism

Rather than being truly pantheistic, the Celts saw the various Goddesses and Gods as energetic aspects of the Mother Goddess, who in the Irish tradition is Dana. Each Goddess and God also has a natural aspect, which again returns to the concept of the sacred land. The Mother Goddess and the Earth—in Celtic shamanism the many Gods and Goddesses were divine aspects of both. Essentially, when ancestors died they became divine aspects of the Goddess, returning to the land from whence they were born, to once again be reborn of the Goddess. They become the sleepers who reside in the land, whose energy can be called upon by future generations.

The Celts observed each cycle or season of the Goddess and God through rituals that followed the path of the sun throughout the year. In this sense, they were sun worshipers who also kept track of the lunar cycles, particularly as to how the lunar related to the solar cycle. This had the very practical result of reminding people when to plant and harvest, but there was also a shamanistic aspect to it. The seasonal festivals and full moon rituals were also a way to observe the various spiritual and energetic aspects of the Goddess and God.

Another concept that relates back to the idea of the Mother

Goddess is the concept of Oneness. Oneness is a divine energy that is in everything. Essentially, in the Celtic cosmology of the world, from out of the Goddess or Oneness came the whole of existence. In the *Gwyddonic Druid Tradition Great Book,* which derives from a Welsh tradition, it says:

> Out of that which has no name issued She who is the Mother of all things. The Greatest One, the Mother of us all did take upon Herself two aspects: One which we call the Dark One, and that which we call the Bright One. This was done so that there would be an ever-renewing of all things, and that all things might ever grow; learning from what has passed before.

This cosmology is consistent with the Egyptian and Greek, in that all the Gods and Goddesses come from or are born from the original "Mother Goddess." In this respect, they are aspects of her. These aspects usually represent or are connected to forces of nature, including animals, rivers, and plants. Examples are Fliodhas, the deer Goddess, and Robur, God of the oaks. This particular concept will be covered more extensively in chapter 2 of this book, "Celtic Gods and Goddesses."

The Sacred and Living Land

Being the embodiment of the Goddess as well as the receptacle of ancestral energy, the land was sacred to the Celts. To them, the land was a living, breathing, and feeling being, who met their physical needs in that she provided them with food, clothing, and shelter. This living being never actually died, but instead was constantly renewed with each year's planting and harvest. In this way, the harvest was never viewed as an end or a death because part of what was harvested were the seeds for next year's planting.

Taking the concept into the spiritual realm, the Celts were

linked to the plants and animals around them. People were born and lived their lives often in one place; when they died, they were buried in the land, where their spirits were renewed or reborn as a divine aspect of the Goddess.

The Irish Druids believed in a type of reincarnation in which souls do not die but pass from one form to another. These forms include not only people, but also animals and inanimate objects such as trees and stones. The Irish looked for immortality in a far-off spirit land in the realm of mystery.

This Druidic belief in reincarnation is viewed as another link and connection between the Druids and the Brahmans in India; it also has ties to the Mediterranean Cult of the Dead. From reincarnation, the Druids derived the concept of transmigration, which is a cycle that takes place in one lifetime or in many, whereby a person assumes the shape of several different animals and inanimate objects and is then reborn. Transmigration is further explored later in this chapter.

In addition, the ancient Druids believed that by burying their dead in sacred groves, the spirit and power of their ancestors would become part of the land. Once this energy merged with the land, it could be drawn upon at any time by anyone who knew how to unlock its secret power. The mythology of King Arthur and the Knights of the Round Table revolves around this concept of the sleeping king, whose power waits to be awakened by those who know the ancient ways and mysteries.

Natural Wisdom

How to connect with the sacred and living land and work with the energies of nature was natural wisdom that the Celts passed on from generation to generation. Besides being tuned in to nature's seasonal changes, they also used natural energies and ley lines in their magical traditions. In the world of the ancient Celts, every detail in the landscape was personified and as a result become spiritual. They gave everything around them life by associating it with a Goddess, a God, an ancestor, and energy. Every place, lake, and grove of trees had a story or number of stories that connected it to the spiritual world of the Celts.

The Celts preserved their spiritual traditions through the Bardic system. Bards carried the mythology of the Celts down through the ages; contained within these myths were the family histories and natural wisdom of each clan and tribe. Celtic Bards were known for their extraordinary ability to memorize stories and songs that often numbered into the hundreds.

In addition, myths were and still are valuable because they offer keys to understanding natural phenomena. They often combine many different types or aspects of knowledge at once. In the context of the ancient Celts, the value of such keys came through ritual, particularly in cases where magic was made in accordance with natural wisdom in the form of observed signs, seasons, and places. This was especially true when the magic was thought to bring fertility and benefit from the Otherworld to human and animal recipients. Although this is an over-simplification of the purpose of ritual, it provides a loose construct for how natural wisdom continued to evolve.

Celtic shamans generally performed their rituals out in nature, usually in a place of power such as a sacred well or spring, a forest clearing, or a hilltop. These places of power were almost always situated on ley lines where there was lots of natural energy. Before rituals and celebrations, the shamans called their ancestral spirits, animal totems, and other energies into the sacred area, increasing the power available for magical works, shape-shifting, and shamanic journeying.

Animal Totems

Many of the Celtic Goddesses and Gods had animal forms or were associated with particular animals. Examples include the

Goddess Morgana, who sometimes took the form of a black raven, and the God Kernunnos, who was often portrayed as a majestic horned stag. Many Irish stories describe the magical abilities and adventures of animals, and many locales in Ireland take their names from animals (for example, the Ox Mountains, Ravendale, and Crow's Valley). Interestingly, the early Irish paid animals the same divine honors as the Egyptians had.

Celtic mythology is full of references to the kindred and magical relationship between people and animals. Not only did people shape-shift and transmigrate into the forms of animals, but there were also stories of people such as the Wild Herdsman in the tale of "The Lady of the Fountain," who were guardians of the animals of the forest and had a spiritual and magical relationship with the spirits of animals. In the story, the wild herdsman is a black giant with a club that he uses to beat on the belly of a stag to gather the animals together. Also, in the earlier texts regarding Merlin, such as *Vita Merlini* (1132), he is shown riding on a stag, acting as a guardian to the totemic forces that inhabit the land.

Different Celtic clans and tribes had totems or spiritual relationships with their animal(s), depending on their particular tradition. Wolves were thought to be mystical creatures and guides to the Otherworld. People from this totem were thought to have the powers of the wolf. People of the boar totem, on the other hand, were thought to be kingly. Often these totems or the use of certain spirit animals related back to the Mother Goddess of that clan or tribe. Rosemarie Anderson depicts this in her book *Celtic Oracles* when she says, "Like Mother Goddesses, carrion birds are complex symbols of death and rebirth. Statuary and coins depicting carrion birds hint at myths and symbols long forgotten by history. At temple shrines dedicated to the Mother Goddess Nantosuelta, ravens perch near her as though bearing messages from the Otherworld."

Some animals such as the hare, revered in Egypt in the form

of the hare-headed deity Dendera, were not eaten by the Celts, but others, like the pig, they had a fondness for. This fondness is said to be derived from the pig's liking for acorns, the produce of the saintly oak. Legends speak of when the Milesians first sought the shores of Ireland, and how the Tuatha De Danann created a magical fog that gave the land the appearance of a large pig, or "Muc Inis," Hog Island.

Deer were another spirit animal that the Celts used in their spiritual traditions. They considered deer magical creatures and felt that the horns protruding from the deer's head were a symbol of powerful life force. This idea harkens back to that of the horned God and also relates to the Celtic belief in the sacred head, that a being's energy resides in the head. In Celtic tradition deer were frequently the means of taking souls to the Otherworld. They were supernatural animals of the fairy world and were fairy cattle and messengers. In Celtic mythology the deer was one of the primary animals used for transformation, usually coming in the form of a white doe or white stag. In this form, the deer came to people who encountered it as an other-worldly messenger that led the people ever deeper into the forest, to realms of unknown and magical wonders and directly to spirit and divine communication.

Shape-Shifting and Transmigration

Shape-shifting and transmigration are ways the ancient Celts furthered their connection with animals. By becoming a particular animal, they assumed its shape and perception and through this experience learned to utilize the power of that animal. Simply put, shape-shifting or metamorphosis refers to shifting into a particular shape, whereas transmigration denotes a cycle of changes and rebirth. In Celtic mythology Merlin provides an example of shape-shifting; transmigration is portrayed in the story about the Goddess Etain.

When shape-shifting, Celtic shamans would begin a journey of perception, setting aside natural laws, such as gravity, while entering a world where they could merge or meld into the body of any animal, plant, rock, or body of water. Shape-shifting was a method by which they became anything they chose, experiencing an entirely different world—the world of instinct. By becoming an eagle, the shaman could fly above the treetops and observe the world as a whole from the sky, instead of seeing things from one location on the ground. By becoming the wolf, a shaman got in touch with his or her wild self while heightening the senses of smell and hearing.

Shape-shifting enabled the Celts to strengthen their ties with their spirit animals and totems. At the moment a person changes form at will, be it physically or experientially, shifting into the shape of a wolf or any animal, it strengthens and reinforces the connection with that animal totem. In this sense, the eagle, raven, boar, wolf—or whatever animal a person, clan, or tribe felt an affinity for—become their animal allies, helpers, and protectors upon whom they could call at any time. By releasing the power and increasing the vitality within themselves, the energy and knowledge of the eagle, wolf, or any creature could be theirs when they needed it.

In Irish mythology, many of the Faeries possessed the power to change into different shapes, depending on the type of Faery. "Spriggans" can alter their size. The "Eash Uisge" have two forms, a young man and a horse, and the Cornish Faeries change into the shape of a bird. Along with the Faeries, the Bogy or Bogey Beasts and the Hobgoblins were true shape-shifters. Traditionally, they exercised their powers for mischief rather than for malevolence. Stories tell of how wizards, particularly supernatural wizards, had the ability to change form at will into other people. The stories also say that wizards could shift from one shape to another at will. One of these shape-shifting wizards of Celtic mythology was Merlin, or Myrddin as he is called in Welsh tradition.

The stories of Merlin and his connection to animals and shape-shifting describe him turning into a variety of animal forms, including a stag and a wolf. In such a tale, Jean Markale, in *Merlin: Priest of Nature,* remarks:

> What characterizes Merlin, as well as the Irish Dagda, is that he is the master of animals. In the *Vita Merlini* he is riding a stag (which is to say that he has taken the form of a stag) and is accompanied by a wolf (which is to say that he is a wolf). To be master of animals is not only to be obeyed by animals but also to be able to assume their forms. And that is pure shamanism.

In mythical times each tribal member could metamorphose into an animal, which meant that everyone was able to share in the condition of the ancestor. Today such intimate relationships with mythical ancestors are reserved exclusively for shamans and other highly skilled metaphysicians.

In Irish traditions, transmigration means the soul's passing from human form into other forms, including both human and animal shapes. To the Greeks, transmigration meant the transformation of one body into another, whereas the Gaelic tales of shape-shifting deal with the transmigration of a soul into the body of another human being. Transmigration indicates that the individual is migrating from one state of being into another, passing at death from one state of existence to another. Transmigration usually includes being born later in human form. Taliesin is an excellent example of this, as seen in the translation of the "Birth of Taliesin" in *Celtic Druids, Celtic Bards* by R. J. Stewart and Robin Williamson:

I have been a blue salmon
A dog, a stag, a roebuck on the mountain
A stick, a spade, an axe in the hand
A buck, a bull, a stallion
Upon a hill I was grown as grain
Reaped and in the oven thrown
Out of that roasting I fell to the ground
Pecked up and swallowed by the black hen
In her crop nine nights lain
I have been dead, I have been alive
I am Taliesin.

In the story of Etain, transmigration occurs and she exists in various forms or stages, which in the end lead to a major transformation, being born a thousand years later. In Etain's story, Midhir's wife, Fuamnach, a sorceress, is extremely jealous of the lovely Etain. She strikes Etain with a rod of scarlet quickentree and casts a spell upon her. Etain suddenly turns into a pool of water. Afterward, the crystal pool dries, rolls itself together, and becomes a small worm. The worm turns into a magical purple fly of wondrous size, and the sweet spray that falls from her wings can cure all sickness. Fuamnach creates a magical wind to blow Etain away, and she is harbored by Angus Og in his sun chamber for some time. Etain finally falls into the cup of wine belonging to the wife of Edar. The woman drinks the wine and Etain is reborn a thousand years after her initial birth.

Transmigration, like shape-shifting, deals with the changing of the outer form, and from this outer physical change comes an inner perceptual transformation. Within this process is the true meaning of shape-shifting and transmigration. This meaning comes from assuming the shape of another. On one hand, you gain a connection with the shape you change into and the wisdom therein, and second, your overall perception of the world changes and you become a different person. The Celts used the arts of shape-shifting and transmigration as a means to actualize both of these experiences.

Spirit Animal and Shape-Shifting Visualization

This section takes you on journey where you shape-shift and become your spirit animal for a few moments. This exercise gives you a basic feeling of how the ancient Celts used shape-shifting and transmigration as tools for personal transformation and to move dimensionally into other worlds or realms of existence. Using the information in this chapter on Celtic roots, imagine yourself out in nature as a Celtic shaman. Use the imagery to go deeper into the experience of the visualization.

For this visualization, find a quiet place to relax, somewhere you will not be disturbed by people, the telephone, or loud external noises. As you read the visualization, actually see and sense yourself going through the experience. To intensify this experience, read this visualization into a tape recorder, using your own voice, beginning and ending the journey with the rhythmic pounding of a drum or rattle. The best time to listen to your visualization is just before you go to sleep and just upon waking, when your mind is most open to new suggestions and experiences.

To connect with your spirit animals of the four directions, begin by focusing your attention on a lit green candle in front of you. I also suggest placing a stone in each of your hands, using tumbled malachite in your left hand and tumbled clear quartz in your right hand. Two river stones or stones you find in nature, one green and one clear or white, work well for this visualization. Also, light some incense or smudge before starting the visualization journey.

As a point of reference, some of the animals common to the Celts were: wolf, cat, dog, fox, rabbit (hare), mouse, dragon, crane, seal, salmon, bear, deer (stag), swan, owl, squirrel, falcon, crow, raven, otter, dog (hound), eagle, swine (boar), horse, and cow (bull). Your spirit animals of the four directions may be of this group or may be creatures from other parts of the world. Go with whatever feels right for you.

Focus on the candle in front of you, merging with the light that radiates from its flame. Look at all of the subtle colors that pour from the flame of the green forest-colored candle. Breathe deeply and completely several times, and imagine yourself pouring all of your tensions, worries, and pains into the flame of the candle. Feel the tensions of the day melting from your body and mind, just as the candle wax melts in the hot flame in front of you.

Slowly close your eyes completely. Notice that they feel so relaxed, they naturally close all by themselves. See and sense yourself standing in a beautiful and very magical forest, with oak, pine, fir, birch, and ash trees surrounding you, forming what looks like a natural circle. Ferns dot the woods, growing over moss-covered boulders. White, red, and gold wild-flowers look like tiny jewels in the forest and large white quartz rocks line the ring of trees, marking the small clearing.

Breathe deeply and completely, using your breath to visualize and sense the small forest clearing. You can hear the sounds of birds in the canopy of trees and crickets in the distance. The smell of the trees, the ground, flowers, and water nearby fill your senses as you listen to the breeze that whispers through the trees like the whispered voices of ancestral spirits, speaking in a natural and ancient language.

A mighty oak stands at the North point of the small forest clearing. The trunk and the sinuous curving of a low branch create a natural altar. Resting on the altar are several magical tools. There is a simple wooden bowl carved from an oak branch, filled with earth, a crystal-tipped wand, a golden sword covered with jewels, and an earth-colored stoneware chalice filled with water.

You study the altar tools for a few moments, drinking in their splendor and magical energy. Then you begin your spirit animal journey by drawing a sacred circle of light around the small clearing in the forest. Slowly see and feel yourself turning around in a clockwise circle with your hands stretched out in front of you. A beautiful blue-white light radiates out from your outstretched hands. This light creates a protective and nourishing circle of radiance that surrounds the clearing in the forest and fills your being. You say silently as you spin around, "May all evil and foulness be gone from this place. I ask this in the Lady's name. Be gone, now and forever more." As you continue to slowly spin around, build the radiant light of the sacred circle with your mind.

Breathe deeply to see the sacred circle and forest more clearly. Bring all of your senses into play in this magical forest. Take the wooden bowl filled with earth from the altar. Begin at the North point, next to the altar, take three pinches of earth from the bowl, and sprinkle them, one at a time, on the ground in front of you. Purify the North point by silently chanting:

"Ayea, Ayea Kerridwen! Ayea, Ayea Kernunnos! Ayea, Ayea, Ayea!"

See and sense yourself moving clockwise to the East point and repeating the process, sprinkling three pinches of the earth on the ground in front of you and silently saying:

"Ayea, Ayea Kerridwen! Ayea, Ayea Kernunnos! Ayea, Ayea, Ayea!"

See and sense yourself moving to the South point and sprinkling three pinches of the earth on the ground in front of you, silently saying:

"Ayea, Ayea Kerridwen! Ayea, Ayea Kernunnos! Ayea, Ayea, Ayea!"

Finish at the West point, repeating the process of slowly sprinkling three pinches of the earth from the bowl onto the ground and silently repeating:

"Ayea, Ayea Kerridwen! Ayea, Ayea Kernunnos! Ayea, Ayea, Ayea!"

Breathe deeply and very gently place the wooden bowl back upon the altar. Thank the spirits of nature for their protection and for sharing their light. Visualize yourself taking the finely crafted crystal-tipped wand from the altar. Hold it in your hands, gazing at its beauty for a moment, and then tap nine times on the surface of the altar of the mighty oak tree with the base of the wand. Set the wand back down upon the altar.

It is now time to call in your spirit animals of the four directions. These spirit animals are your totems, your guardians, protecting the directions of your sacred circle. They are your friends, helping you in the spirit world and in all dimensions, including the physical world. Your spirit animals are your special totem companions in dreaming. They can help you actualize your deepest dreams.

Standing at the North point in front of the altar, begin by taking the bowl of earth in your hands. Hold it up in front of you and merge with the powers of the Earth. Visualize and sense the Earth and its soil, the rocks underground and above ground, the trees, and the lush vegetation of the forest. Smell the earthiness of the forest floor and allow your gaze to focus on the North point of the forest clearing. See and sense yourself lifting the bowl of earth upward and silently saying:

"Oh, great and mighty one, spirit animal of the North March, come, I pray you. Enter the gate of the North Ward and make yourself clearly known to me. Come, I ask you to share your wisdom of the powers of Earth with me!"

Set the wooden bowl back down on the altar and wait a few moments, taking a deep breath and calming your mind a little more.

You will begin to notice, at the corner of the North point, an animal moving toward you. You feel no fear and welcome your spirit animal of the North. Study the animal and greet it. Reach out very slowly and touch your spirit animal. As you touch, feel the spirit animal enter your heart, the very core of your being, and speak to you with the voice of the universe. If you have a particular question to ask, do so now, and listen for the reply. Dance, walk, run, or sit for a minute with your spirit animal. Shape-shift for a moment or two into your spirit animal, feeling what it is like to be in its body, better understanding how the spirit animal thinks and feels. Become one with your spirit animal of the North. Allow yourself to journey with your spirit animal for a few moments, noticing something of interest along the way.

Now thank your spirit animal of the North and watch as it moves back to the northern corner of the clearing, slowly shimmering and fading from your vision. Pick up the wand from the natural altar set in the mighty oak tree and move in a clockwise circle to the East point. Merge with the powers of Air, holding the wand high in the air and silently saying:

"Oh, great and mighty one, spirit animal of the East March, come, I pray you. Enter the gate of the East Ward and make yourself clearly known to me. Come, I ask you to share your wisdom of the powers of Air with me!"

You see another animal, a different spirit animal, coming toward you from the East point. Again, there is no fear and you welcome your spirit animal of the East. Reach out and make contact with the animal and feel its essence and knowledge merging with yours, entering your heart and communicating with the voice of the universe. Ask a question of this spirit friend and listen closely to the animal's reply. Breathe deeply to help you listen and absorb your spirit animal's message completely. Dance, walk, fly, or crawl for a few moments with your spirit animal of the East, shape-shifting for a few moments into the animal itself. Become one with your spirit animal of the East and the powers of Air. Sense yourself journeying with your spirit animal for a few moments and notice something of interest along your journey.

Thank your spirit animal of the East and watch as it shimmers and then fades back into the eastern corner of the clearing in the thick woods. See yourself moving over to the natural oak altar and pick up the ornate, jewel-covered, golden sword. It feels very heavy and amazingly warm in your hands. Move opposite the altar to the South point and merge with the powers of the creative Fire, and while holding the sword upward and out, silently say:

> "Oh, great and mighty one, spirit animal of the South March, come, I pray you. Enter the gate of the South Ward and make yourself clearly known to me. Come, I ask you to share your wisdom of the powers of the creative Fire with me!"

Set the golden sword back on the altar and quietly wait.

Watching the southern corner of the forest clearing very closely, you will see the outline of an animal coming toward you. Without fear, greet your spirit animal of the South and the powers of Fire. As you touch, you feel the warmth of the spirit animal enter your heart and you are filled with its essence and the ancient knowledge of the powers of the creative Fire. Communicate with the animal and ask one question. Breathe deeply as you wait for the spirit animal's reply. Begin to dance, sing, or run with your spirit animal of the South for a few moments, shape-shifting into the animal. Gently allow yourself to feel what it is like being this animal for a few moments. Travel with your spirit animal for a few moments and as you journey, notice something of interest. Thank your spirit animal of the South and then watch as it slowly shimmers and disappears from your sight in the South point of the forest.

Go to the natural altar, under the mighty oak, once again, and pick up the earthen-colored chalice of water from its surface. Move to the West point and merge with the powers of Water. Silently say:

> "Oh, great and mighty one, spirit animal of the West March, come, I pray you. Enter the gate of the West Ward and make yourself clearly known to me. Come, I ask you to share your wisdom of the powers of the primal Waters with me!"

Set the chalice back down on the altar and wait very quietly.

Suddenly, you begin to see an animal in the depths of the woods, coming into the clearing and toward you from the West. Again, there is no fear and you welcome your spirit animal of the powers of Water. Reach out and make contact with the animal and feel its essence and knowledge, entering your heart and communicating with the voice of the universe. Ask a question of this Water spirit friend and listen closely to the animal's reply. Swim, dance, or dream for a few moments with your spirit animal of the West, shape-shifting for a few moments into the animal itself. Become one with your watery spirit animal of the West. Take a few moments to travel with your spirit animal and notice something of interest while doing so.

Thank your Water spirit animal and watch as it shimmers and fades into the west corner of the deep, thick forest. See and sense yourself moving back to the natural altar that is set into the mighty oak tree. Thank your spirit animals of the four directions for their kinship, protection, and knowledge. Send a last silent farewell to each of them, knowing that you can communicate with them whenever you choose by simply asking them to be present and help you in your daily life. Give thanks to the Great Mother and All Father before you pull up your sacred circle of light.

See and feel yourself extending your hands in front of you and spinning slowly in a counterclockwise circle, visualizing the radiant blue-white light of the circle being drawn into the palms of your hands. As the light moves into your palms, you feel and sense the healing energy flowing through your entire being, energizing you.

See and feel yourself taking the magical crystal-tipped wand from the altar, one last time. Slowly and firmly knock on the natural altar three times with the base of the crystal-tipped wand. Set the wand back down upon the altar and look around at the thick forest that surrounds you. You feel comfortable and safe in the deep woods, knowing that the animals and all of nature's spirits are there to protect and guide you in the forest and in your daily life.

Breathe deeply and begin to come back to the room, repositioning your body and moving your legs, feet, arms, and hands around, and finally returning to the room and the present moment completely. Open your eyes and take a few minutes to ponder over your experience. Jot down what your spirit animals are for the four directions, any messages you received, and anything you noticed in your journey. I suggest you keep a journal or notebook in which to write your experiences. Allow the candle to burn all the way down.

2

CELTIC GODS
AND GODDESSES

I was in many shapes before I was released:
I was a slender, enchanted sword—I believe
    that it was done.
I was rain-drops in the air, I was stars' beam;
I was a word in letters, I was a book in origin;
I was lanterns of light for a year and a half;
I was a bridge that stretched over sixty estuaries;
I was a path, I was an eagle, I was a coracle in seas;
I was a bubble in beer, I was a drop in a shower;
I was a sword in hand, I was a shield in battle
I was a string in a harp enchanted nine years,
    in the water as foam;
I was a spark in fire, I was wood in a bonfire;
I am not one who does not sing; I have sung
    since I was small.

From the "Cad Goddeu,"
from the *Book of Taliesin*

The Mother Goddess

As the symbol of creation, who embodied the eternal cycle of birth, life, and death (rebirth), the Goddess was a fundamental and universal power to the ancient Celts. She wove all dimensions and energies together into a Oneness. She acted as the supreme regulator of all life, for she controlled the seasons, the cycles of nature, and the movement of the sun, moon, and all celestial bodies.

The idea that the Goddess embodies and is One with the sacred land forms the fundamental foundation of Celtic spirituality. To the Celts, she offered the promise of wholeness because her knowledge came through the heart and touched the spirit. By communing and connecting with nature, they felt the power of the Goddess, which was essential to the fertility and continuance of the annual cycles. Their survival depended on being connected to this power rather than separate from it. This is why so much of Celtic spirituality stems from the Celts' relationship with the Goddess and all her faces.

The Celtic Gods and Goddesses are aspects of the Mother Goddess. In this context, Celtic spiritual traditions were, and still are, paradoxically both monotheistic and polytheistic. The traditions have a tendency toward monotheism in their reverence for the Mother Goddess and in the way various Celtic Gods and Goddesses represent the many aspects and forces that make up the Goddess as a whole. An example of this is the Celtic God Llyr, God of the sea. The sea is a particular force or aspect of the whole of nature. Llyr, as the sea God, was a way for the Celts to perceive the sea as alive, containing characteristics of its own. By personifying the sea, the Celts had an active relationship with the sea and the spirits therein. They imbued it with divine and immortal life. At the same time, holistically, the sea is one of the many forces of nature and in turn the Goddess and the feminine.

From the original Mother Goddess stemmed the many

aspects that became Gods and Goddesses of the Celtic pantheon. This mirrors nature. In a sense, it is an ancient form of divine cloning, whereby the Goddess keeps giving a piece of herself and in the process creates another divine being. Interestingly, incarnation is still a concept that is taught in modern Celtic traditions.

Through time, the polytheistic nature of Celtic faith predominated, particularly as different Celtic clans and tribes worshiped their own sets of Gods and Goddesses. But the primary concept is the idea of the Mother Goddess and how the other Gods and Goddesses resonate or come alive through her. One way this takes place is by virtue of each Goddess and God, beginning with the Mother Goddess and Father God, having three basic aspects, or faces; some say nine. These faces represent the many qualities of natural energies and they mirror human characteristics. One way to know deity, to connect with spirit, is to look into your own mirrored face.

The Triple Goddess

A mythological and metaphysical paradigm centers around the idea that deity, in order to experience itself, splits, clones, births, or creates the other by some other means. Deity does this in order to experience its own divinity. The other provides a mirror. Essentially, the Mother Goddess does the same, in that each of her aspects adds to her overall form. Instead of a vague, ambiguous one-dimensional image, she takes shape as a real being in the three-dimensional world, as evidenced by her three faces: maid, mother, and crone. Each of the many aspects of the Mother Goddess are reflections of the whole, of her totality, and of Oneness.

The Triple Goddess draws upon the idea that the Mother Goddess symbolizes both feminine and masculine energies. In a desire to know herself better, she split into two (Goddess and God) and, in doing so, gained more knowledge about herself through the other. Henceforth, the God embodied her male aspects or faces, and the Goddess represented her female qualities.

Between the two polarities, there exists a neutral zone, symbolizing the polar balance that the Chinese call the "Tao," the presence of being in which the two poles meet and essentially become One. Many spiritual systems, including the Celtic traditions and Wicca, refer to this meeting of the poles as a divine or magical experience, a crossroads of spiritual energies and dimensions.

Early Celtic peoples viewed all life as existing on three integrated levels: body, mind, and spirit. Within each being, spirit acted as the unifying force, weaving together all levels of existence. The Celts symbolized this concept of Oneness with the triple spiral or triple knot. That which cannot be explained by conscious logic can often be accounted for in the ever-present, unseen realms of spirit. In the oneness of being, no part can be greater or lesser. In Celtic traditions, true vision of spirit and divine ecstasy can only be achieved when you find the central harmony of body, mind, and spirit.

Various Celtic traditions use the Threefold One to describe the trinity of energy of the Three Worlds: the Otherworlds of ancestors and Faeries, the Earth they live upon, and the Upperworld of the sky. The Mother Goddess has two sides, one bright and one dark, and each of these sides has three aspects or faces, meaning that all things, whether bright or dark, have a beginning, middle, and end; youth, middle age, and old age; positive, neutral, and negative; birth, life, and death. The Goddess directs all things in this cycle: dormant, the greening, and harvest.

The sacredness of the number three is crucial to understanding the spiritual traditions of the Goddess. This threefold nature reflects in the way the Goddess is worshiped in her three aspects of maiden, mother, and crone, and the God in his three faces of son, father, and wise man. These three aspects of the Goddess and God link directly to the phases of the moon, the Wheel of the Year, and the Three Worlds.

The maiden embodies woman as a virgin, when her powers collect and grow stronger. As mother, she becomes fertile, releasing her stored energies and exchanging energy with her partners and children. The third aspect, that of hag or crone, is a woman who acts as the dissipator of energy. Hag stems from the Greek *hagia,* which means "holy one." As crone or hag, a woman becomes holy and wise when she no longer sheds the lunar wise blood.

The Goddess Triana is an example of the Triple Goddess and the Threefold One. As Sun-Ana, she is the maiden, the Daughter Goddess of healing, knowledge, and mental arts. She becomes the Mother Goddess of nature, life, and death as Earth-Ana. As Moon-Ana, she acts as the Crone Goddess of higher love and wisdom.

The son represents the virginal male, growing stronger and more directed. As father, he becomes virile and joins with the mother in the cycle of renewal through sexual union. As wise man, he disseminates his knowledge and skills to others for the use of future generations.

The triple form of Celtic Goddesses and Gods stems from a concept that seems to have its roots in Indo-European peoples. It also relates to the Hindu idea of the Trimurti, which consisted of Brahma (the Creator), Vishnu (the Preserver), and Shiva (the Destroyer). In another connection, Pythagoras saw three as the perfect number of the philosophers—the beginning, middle, and end—and he used the triune as a symbol of deity. The Greek tradition saw the world ruled by three primary Gods: Zeus (the celestial realms), Poseidon (the sea), and Pluto/Hades (the Underworld).

The Celts perceived their world in triple form also. They saw people as composed of body, soul, and spirit; the world composed of earth, sea, and air; and nature composed of animal, vegetable, and mineral. The ancient Druids designated the number three as the number of all things and they taught in sequences of three, called triads. Combinations of the figure three occur often in Celtic tales, including the numbers nine (three times three), thirty-three, and eighty-one.

The Goddess and Her Consort

Accounts in Irish mythology state that no mortal king could assume true sovereignty at Tara without first coupling with one of the Goddesses of the land. For example, the Queen of Connacht, Medb, cohabited with nine kings. The Goddess or Queen in her role as a woman was viewed as the source of creation and thus the creator of the human species as a whole, with her main role the progenitor of life. The ancient Celts viewed the relationship between the Goddess and God in terms of feminine and male archetypes.

Early Celts perceived the sun to be a feminine symbol, renewed every year at Yule and progressing through the year from that point. The Celts considered woman the source of creation, and from her womb and body came all life. Originally, she was the Sun, Moon, Earth, and Stars. Only later, when Roman and Christian influences came into play, did the whole cosmology get translated into paternal terms and the Sun became male. The Sun deity went from being a Goddess (female) to being a God (male). This unnatural alteration, substituting male for female, not only created an enormous energetic imbalance, but effectively devalued women, stealing their power and light, making sovereignty of the land a concept of the past, and hence ignorantly exploiting the Earth's resources.

Initially, as the Sun became a symbol of masculinity, the solar God was seen as the consort of the Goddess, whose symbol was the Earth. The path of the consort (Sun) was viewed in terms of his effect on the land, an example being that longer and warmer days occurred between the spring equinox and the summer solstice, which facilitated plants' germinating and growing. The important thing is that the feminine and the Goddess were paramount to survival; the male and God aspect had a supporting role.

Celtic Solar Festivals

The Celtic festivals and Great Days follow the Goddess and God as they travel the path of the Sun, turning with the Great Wheel of the Year. These festivals mark the effects and changes that this turning has on the Earth and Goddess. The Sun is not reborn each year with the coming of spring; it is the Earth who comes alive each spring and from whose womb springs the infinite creation of life. From this perspective, the Great Days are celebrations of the Mother Goddess and her relationship and rapport with the Sun (God). Some of the Great Days, such as Bridget's Day, Hertha's Day (spring equinox), and Hellith's Day (autumnal equinox), take their names from the seasonal faces of the Goddess and God.

The Goddess anchored her mate's nature, like her own, to the rotations of the skies, the seasons, and the cycles, so that after the winter solstice (Yule), their bright natures would begin to awaken, growing stronger and more vital on the spring equinox. The bright natures of the Goddess and God rule the season of the greening. After the harvest comes the time for the dark natures of the Goddess and God to rule and roam the land freely while their bright natures enter dormancy and winter sleep, reawakening once again in the spring.

Seasonal solar and lunar rituals and celebrations act as the symbolic bodily expression of the ancient and boundless love between the Goddess and the God. The Moon is a reflection of the Sun. In the Gwyddonic Druid tradition, an initiatory Druid path I am familiar with, there is a saying, "Perfect Love and Perfect Peace." First, it means the perfect love of the Goddess and the perfect peace of the God. Second, it means the perfect love of knowledge and the perfect peace of wisdom. Third, it means the perfect love of all Nature and perfect peace by being in harmony with all things, whether animate or inanimate.

Many Celtic traditions, particularly Celtic Wicca, see Samhain as the beginning of the year, and some, such as the one I was trained in, see Yule as the beginning of the year. The reason some traditions believe Yule, also called "Alban Arthuan" by Druids, to be the beginning of Celtic year is because this Great Day occurs on the winter solstice, the time when the light cycle changes and the days begin getting longer. The word *Yule* comes from the Norse word for "wheel," eliciting the image of the Celtic "Wheel of the Year" with its eight spokes, denoting the four major agricultural and pastoral festivals as well as the four minor solar festivals of the solstices and equinoxes. The basic mythology behind Yule revolves around the idea that the Sun, and in turn the Earth, is reborn, beginning once again the annual cycle of life. As the Sun came to symbolize the Sun God, consort to the Goddess, the traditional festivals and rituals of Yule honored the rebirth of the consort and in turn the Mother Goddess herself, called by the names of Dana, Danu, Anu, and Kerridwen.

The Yule ritual starts just before midnight and ends shortly after midnight. The rebirth of the Sun God is represented by a lighted, live evergreen tree. In the past, the live tree was decorated with candles; now electric lights are most frequently used. Three women, representing the three aspects of the maiden, mother, and crone, light the candles. Other Yule traditions include the Yule log and the Yule candle. The Yule log was a means to receive the blessing of the Sun. The collecting, hauling, and kindling of the wood for the Yule log was done in a ritualistic manner. The Celts believed that a piece of the Yule log, if kept safe, would protect the house, secure a bountiful harvest, and aid the livestock in birthing. The Yule candle was a very large ornamental candle, usually blue, green, or red in color, lit at the beginning of the Yule season.

Between the winter solstice and spring equinox, in the early part of February, is Bridget's Fire, also known as Imbolc and Oimelg. This festival and Great Day is the point in the seasonal cycle when the first lambing takes place, along with the female sheep or ewes coming into milk. To the Celts, the first sheep's milk was important because it came at a time in the annual cycle (winter) when no other fresh food was available. Fire is also an important element on this Great Day, symbolizing the first signs of life being rekindled. This is also the time when some early flower bulbs begin showing signs of life.

Bridget's temple was the sanctuary of the sacred fire, which was never allowed to burn out except once each year. Traditionally, across the Celtic countryside, households also let their fires die out only on Bridget's Eve. The next morning, the High Priestess lit a new fire, called the "need-fire," out of nine types of wood, and afterward the women from the households would come to Bridget's temple and gather the sacred fire. They would light a branch from the fire, take it home, and start their hearth fires. As they lit their fires, they chanted:

"Bridget, Bridget, Bridget, brightest flame. Bridget, Bridget, Bridget, sacred name!"

Another tradition closely associated with Bridget's Fire is the planting of fruit trees as a symbol of the fruitful and fertile Goddess. In a ritual performed on the Isle of Man, the head of the household would ask a family member to wait outside the front of the house, holding a potted fruit tree. At this point, the other family members who were inside the house called out:

"Bridget, Bridget, Bridget, come to my house, come to my house tonight. Open the door for Bridget, and let Bridget come in."

Then the person outside knocked three times loudly, and the door was opened and the fruit tree brought inside. For the evening, the fruit tree was treated with reverence, and on the next morning, Bridget's Fire, the family planted the tree outside.

As the Sun continues its journey through the solar year, the next festival occurs on the spring equinox, where the light of day has increased, finally equalling the number of hours consumed in the darkness of night. The Gwyddonic tradition calls it Hertha's Day after the Welsh Goddess of rebirth and healing; the Druids call it "Alban Eiler" after the German Celtic Goddess of spring, and a variety of other Celtic traditions call it Ostara, who was both an early Teutonic Goddess of spring and an even earlier Aryan Goddess of the dawn. With a rabbit as an escort, Ostara, whose name in Old English translates to Oestre, was the pagan Goddess whose name still lives on in the modern festival of Easter.

A planting and fertility festival, the spring equinox is a celebration of the end of winter and the beginning of spring. Celts perform rituals associated with fertility and rebirth, and both rabbits and decorated eggs are traditional Celtic symbols of this, surviving into the modern era. In Wales, rituals on this Great Day were followed by the ceremonial planting of seeds. In the Celtic story of Tarvos, the spring equinox represents the time when the golden bull is reborn after his winter's sleep. To people who relied on the cultivation of crops, this was a time for planting seeds and was seen as another turning point in the cycle. The Mother Goddess displays her face of fertility in the spring, symbolizing the re-emergence of life from its winter slumber.

Besides Samhain, Beltane (Beltaine) probably ranks as the second most important Celtic festival not linked to a solstice or equinox. Known in the modern vernacular as May Day, Beltane is the time when strands of May flowers are strung in celebration of the Goddess and worn by the May Queen and King. It is a time of much excitement; the name *Beltane* means the "fires of Bel." As the Celtic God of the rising sun, Bel (Bilé, Belenos, etc.) is a masculine aspect of the Mother Goddess, symbolizing the birth and vigor of life. After being born on the spring equinox, life progresses to the point of being young and playful, which is the essence of Beltane.

Beltane play and practices include dancing around the Maypole and also the crowning of the May Queen and King, who literally and figuratively represent the Goddess and God. The Beltane bonfire is traditional and is lit from a spark emitted by friction or flint. Once lit, people dance the Celtic Holy Round, clockwise around the sacred bonfire. The ancient Celts would drive their cattle through the fire in order to increase the fertility of the herds and prevent disease. Also, rowan or oak branches and twigs are carried three times, sunwise, around the Beltane bonfire for protection and to bring good fortune. Overall, Beltane is a very sensual and blatantly sexual festival because it represents the time when spring has come into full bloom, and all the people, animals, and plants are beginning their mating cycle, making it a celebration of the fertility and renewal of all nature.

On the morning of the summer solstice when the sun rises, the "Shining One," dressed in a robe of bird feathers, walks through the ancient stone avenue on the Isle of Lewis in the Outer Hebrides. The cuckoo, bird of Tir na N'Org, heralds the Shining One's arrival on the longest day of the year. Also known as Alban Heruin, Letha's Day, and Fae Day, Midsummer is usually a more subdued holiday; this is a day when people give their respect to those Fae they have allied with as well as honor the Faeries and those in the Otherworld. Gifts of desserts and wine are left out for the Faery, and the feast includes some favorite foods of the Faeries such as milk, honey, and sweets. Aid is given and received between humans and the Faeries on this day, and Midsummer is a good day to form new alliances with the Faeries because it is on this day that they often show themselves.

As the intermediate point between the planting and harvest, the summer solstice is the longest day of the year and marks the time when the days begin getting shorter, symbolizing the death of the Sun. Also known as Alban Heruin and Litha's Day, after the Saxon flower goddess of Midsummer whose name means "death," this festival was always one of fire, when bonfires burned all night to encourage the Sun, and in turn the consort to the Goddess, to return again in the course of the solar cycle.

A harvest festival, Lughnassad commemorates the wedding feast of Lugh, Celtic God of the setting Sun, to the beautiful Rosemerta, who is the Rose Mother. Nassad means "to give in marriage." Essential foods for the feast include grain products, cakes, and breads as well as autumn fruits and vegetables. Ale, mead, and juice are appropriate Lughnassad beverages. Common colors associated with Lughnassad are the harvest colors of yellow, gold, brown, rust, and orange and, traditionally, the ritual was held just after sunset on the eve of the Great Day. At Teltown on the river Boyne, an ancient Celtic festival occurred commemorating Lugh's foster mother, Taillte, a Goddess of the land and sovereignty. Lughnassad is a memorial to her death and her symbolic rebirth. At "the Hollow of the Fair" couples entered into ceremonial marriages, lasting a year and a day. Their union symbolized the mating of the Earth and Sun, Goddess and God.

Held at the beginning of August, the Lughnassad ritual marks the time when the forces of light and dark converge. Two portals occur, one just prior to sunset and one immediately after the sun goes down. In ancient times, if it rained during this ritual and festival, the participants believed that Lugh himself was present. There was also a prevalence of horses at the fairs associated with Lughnassad, reflecting the association in lore of Lugh and his companion, a white steed. At this time of year, the ground was finally hard enough for some serious horse racing.

Another name for Lughnassad is Lammas, the Saxon Feast of Bread. This feast is the first of the grain harvest and is consumed in ritual loaves. This aspect relates to the shamanic death and transformation of Lugh, who in the Irish tradition is Lleu. In addition, this shamanic use of death as a transformation tool can be compared to that of the Barley God, who is the focus of the traditional folk song "John Barleycorn."

Starting after sunset on the eve of the autumnal equinox, this Great Day is called by several names, including Hellith's Day, Inning, Modron, Alban Elved, the Kern, and Fomhair, which is the Irish Gaelic word for "harvest." Essentially a mirrored image of the spring equinox, the autumnal equinox, on one hand, marks the time before the days grow shorter and the nights grow longer; but on the other hand, this festival celebrates the season's harvest and people begin the necessary process of collecting seeds for the next growing cycle.

In the Hellith's Day rituals, the God symbolized the dying Sun and the last harvests of the season before the cold of winter, but in this death is rebirth and movement through time. Rather than being merely an ending and a beginning, Hellith's Day becomes an extension of the world as a whole, which the Celts viewed as being circular instead of linear, with no beginning or end. With this, death does not really exist but instead acts as a transition point, moving into other dimensions. This is one reason why the Celts used the Great Day festivals as vehicles for moving into the Otherworlds of their Goddesses and

Gods, Faeries, and ancestors. As a result, the festivals nudged them into spiritual harmony with their world.

The Irish word for "summer's end," Samhain occurs at the beginning of November and was believed by the Celts to be when the veil between this world and the Otherworlds is the thinnest, thus allowing people and spirits to move freely between the worlds. The modern festival of Halloween or All Hallow's Eve still retains this belief, as is illustrated by people's wearing of masks and carving of pumpkins as a means of scaring or keeping away unwanted spirits of those who have crossed over from the other side. In many Celtic traditions, Samhain is the beginning of the new year and the time when the Pleiades stars rise, signaling the end of the growing season and the beginning of the Earth's and the Goddess's dormancy period, which lasts until the winter's solstice and the beginning of the cycle of light.

Celtic legends convey the story that on this festival day, the Great Sea Mother, the Morrigan, made love with the Good God, the Dagda, at a forge where two rivers came together. Two customs or rituals associated with Samhain include the "Oracle of Death" and the "Dumb Supper." In the first one, the Druids would draw lots and choose a person to serve as the "Oracle of Death." This person would then merge with the Goddess and answer any questions about the future. In the "Dumb Supper," or feast for the spirits, food and drink were piled on plates, which were then set outside in the dark of night with lit red and white candles surrounding the plate. The next morning, any food or drink still on the plate was given back to the Earth and the Goddess.

Divine Families or Lineages

The Celtic Gods and Goddesses mirror the Celts themselves, particularly with the importance of ancestry and lineage. Part of this mirroring is due to the Gods and Goddesses being ancestors of the Celtic tribes. The stories and mythologies were a way for the various Celtic clans and tribes to remember their ancestors and track their lineages. Another consideration is that not only have the Gods and Goddesses descended from the Mother Goddess, but each Celt has also stemmed from her. A definite kinship existed between mortals and deities. These connections gave an added dimension that is evident in the deep rapport the Celts had with their Gods and Goddesses. This rapport led to their success in the magical and creative arts, as well as their communion with the spiritual and mystical realms.

There seems to be some confusion about whether the Celts saw themselves as having originally descended from the maternal Goddess or the paternal God. This is because at a certain point after the Roman invasion, the Celts inserted their perception of a "Mother Goddess" as the source of their existence into a patriarchal mode of expression. An example is the Celtic God Bilé, who is akin to Bel and Belenus and in certain stories is referred to as the father of Gods and humankind and also Danu's consort. But as Peter Ellis points out in his book *The Druids:*

> The Dagda is portrayed more often than Donn or Bilé as the "father of the Gods." The significance of this is because the Dagda is Danu's son by Bilé. Therefore, Danu still takes precedence as the primary source of life. As the sacred "waters from heaven," Danu watered the oak, which was Bilé, the male fertility symbol, and gave birth to the Dagda, the good god, who fathered the rest of the gods.

Knowing the Celtic people's early reverence for woman's power of creation and the fact that Danu was originally called the "Mother Goddess," the key concept here being "Mother," it is probable that the Celts initially saw themselves as offspring of the Goddess. From the "Mother Goddess" came all the other various lineages of the Celtic Gods and Goddesses. Often the relationships between the deities were interlinked and sometimes incestuous, such as between the brother and sister Gwydion and Arianrhod, which produced Lugh, making Gwydion both his father and his uncle. Although taboo in contemporary society, the union between sister and brother was considered the most sacred union possible by the ancient Mystery Traditions.

The Tuatha De Danann

All Celtic traditions have a deep and enduring connection to the Tuatha De Danann, who later become the Gods and Goddesses of Celtic Mythology. The children of Danu, the Tuatha, are the roots of a tree whose branches spread far and wide, an indication of the popularity and success of their spiritual teachings.

The Tuatha De Danann were the ancient inhabitants of Ireland and the divine race of people in Old Irish mythology, often called the "Shining Ones," who loved and married human beings and later became the mythological Goddesses and Gods of Ireland and the British Isles. They were descendants of Nemed, who dwelled for a time in the Northern Isles of Greece and traveled to Egypt and Asia, coming to the British Isles before 1500 B.C.

Said to have come down from the eastern sky in a cloud of mist to the shores of Ireland, the Tuatha De Danann arrived in Ireland on May Day morning. May Day, also called Beltane, is one of the eight powerful Great Days that occur every year. *The Book of Invasions* says of the Tuatha, "Their intelligence and skills make it likely that they came from the heavens." They brought their magical knowledge, science, and Druidism with them. They also brought four magical objects, representing the four elements: the Stone of Fal, or destiny; the invincible spear and victory lance; the infallible Sword of Light; and the inexhaustible cauldron of plenty.

From the scholarly works of Jean Markale and Zecharia Sitchin, it has been suggested that the Tuatha De Danann were the embodiment of the fabled Hyperboreans, who were linked with the mysterious isle of Thule and lived beyond the North Wind. For instance, the spear of the Tuatha De Danann solar God Lugh came from Assal, one of the northern Hyperborean islands. The Hyperboreans resided on the islands at the northernmost outreaches of civilization, on the horizon where the stars reach the end of their orbits. Dwelling in sacred woods and forests, the Hyperboreans were reputed to be very wise and knowledgeable in astronomy and magic. The fertile islands, with six-month-long days and nights, were home to Hyperborean griffins. These animals were said to be engendered from "another world" and tales of shape-shifting abounded, such as the crane turning from bird into human.

The mythical Hyperborean islands were also the birth place of Leto (Apollo's mother), and the Hyperborean peoples initiated solar sects at both Stonehenge and Delphi, which explains the reason they honored Apollo and many other solar gods, such as Bel (Beli). Callanish, the stone circle on the Island of Lewis that forms the unique shape of a Celtic cross, may have been a "Winged Hyperborean Temple."

The Celtic Druids owe many aspects of their spirituality to their predecessors, particularly the Hyperboreans and the legendary Tuatha De Danann. Some suggest that the Tuatha De Danann were the ones who built the stone circles and observatories, such as Stonehenge, and that the race of Cymry and the Teutones were their descendants, but this means that the Tuatha arrived in the British Isles much earlier, around 3000 B.C.

Conquered and enslaved by the Gaels, the Tuatha De Danann merged with the land. They now reside in Otherworlds—in secret dwelling places, within the stars, within the land, and inside hills, mounds, rivers, and lakes—and also embody the celestial forms of stars, planets, and moons.

The Goddesses and Gods of the Tuatha are reflections of

Oneness, consisting of pure energy, yet each of them has a unique identity and face. They are beings in a merged state, who have transcended ordinary reality. The Tuatha are our divine family and multidimensional friends. They offer love and wisdom. Their energies and qualities incarnate in many of us, lifetime after lifetime, in an effort to bring light and love back to the sacred land.

The works of Zecharia Sitchin also suggest, in conjunction with the oral tradition itself and volumes of folklore and historical references, that it is probable that the tales of the mysterious Anunnaki are akin to aspects of Druidism. Written on the ancient Sumerian clay tablets and recorded in ancient Babylonian mythology, the Anunnaki were the children or followers of An (Anu, Ana), and also the star or sky Gods that came down to the Earth. An was the Sky God and creator of the star spirits of the great Sumerian triad of Anu, Enlil, and Ea. The Sumerian Male Anu parallels the female Tuatha De Danann Anu, Ana, and Danu. In Druidism, Anu is considered the Mother of the Gods, from whom all other Gods stem. During Gwyddonic ritual, I have always heard her called "Anu," rarely Danu.

Bel (Beli, Bilé) is the firstborn son (sun) of Anu of the Tuatha De Danann and parallels the great Mesopotamian God Bel. The word *Danann* is often shown as D'Anann, meaning "of An," again linking the Sky God "An" together with the Tuatha Goddess "Anu." Keep in mind that both masculine and feminine characteristics were ascribed to the ancient Gods. Both Goddesses and Gods were solar, lunar, stellar, and planetary, and often had a combination of these aspects.

The Celtic Pantheon of Goddesses and Gods

To the Irish, the Mother Goddess is Danu. The concept of the Mother Goddess remains the same but has become culturalized as it moved from clan to clan, tribe to tribe. Because there are different Celtic traditions, which encompass everything from the Druidism to the Faery to Wicca, it means that sometimes the various Celtic traditions view a particular Goddess or God differently, depending on the tradition. Even though some of the characteristics and attributes of the Gods and Goddesses changed, many archetypical concepts such as the "Mother Goddess" were universal throughout Celtic traditions.

In Celtic mythology everyone is related to everyone else in some way or another. This mirrors Celtic philosophy. The Celts felt that everything, everyone, every world was interrelated and part of a Oneness, with knowledge itself stemming from the cauldron of the Mother Goddess. The best example of this is depicted in the Four Branches of the Mabinogi: Pwyll, Branwen, Manawydan, and Math.

Pwyll was the Prince of Dyfed and the son of Meirig, who was the son of Arcol, who was the son of Pyr of the East, who was the son of Llion the ancient. Pwyll changed places with the Lord of Annwn, the Otherworld. He married Rhiannon, and their son was called Pryderi. Pryderi was snatched from his bed by a monstrous claw, but his mother, Rhiannon, was accused of murdering him. Rhiannon was forced into servitude at the horse-block. Pryderi was found in a stable by Teirnyon on May Eve and was raised as his own son. When Teirnyon saw the incredible likeness between the boy and the Prince of Dyfed, he returned the boy to his parents and Rhiannon from her servitude. Manawyddan became Pryderi's stepfather and later rescued him from the Otherworld. Pryderi later challenged Gwydion to single combat, and Gwydion came out the victor.

Manawyddan was the son of the sea God Llyr and corresponds to the Irish Manannan mac Llyr, who is considered one of the Tuatha De Danann, although he may be of greater antiquity. He was brother of Bran the Blessed. Upon Bran's death, he was left without land and married Rhiannon. He was foster father to Lugh and guardian of the Isle of Arran and the Isle of

Man. He is mentioned as one of the Grail guardians with Pryderi in the Nennius. Manannan was a master shape-shifter, often shifting into the form of a heron or sea bird, and is associated with stellar navigation. In the *Vita Merlini*, he is the one who ferries King Arthur, Merlin, and Taliesin to the Otherworld.

Llyr was the father of Manawyddan, Bran, Branwen, Efnissien, and Nissien. Llyr is also called Lludd Llaw Ereint, or Silver Hand, making him akin to Nuada and Nodens.

The daughter of Llyr, Branwen, married Matholwch, King of Ireland, and their son was Gwern. She was treated badly by her husband and so got word to her brother Bran by taming a starling to bear a message to him, with Bran then coming from Britain to rescue her. Efnissien killed Branwen's son Gwern by throwing him upon the fire, and after the battle between Ireland and Britain, Branwen died of a broken heart and was buried in Anglessey. The only ones left alive in Ireland after the battle were five pregnant women, who then repopulated the land.

The fourth branch of the Mabinogi is Math, son of Mathonwy, brother of Penardun. He was a great king and uncle to Arianrhod, Gwydion, and Gilfaethwy. When he was not on the battlefield, his feet were resting in the lap of a virgin footholder. Math married his footholder, Goewin, after she was raped by Gilfaethwy and punished his nephews Gilfaethwy and Gwydion by shape-shifting them into animals for a designated period of time. It was Math who eventually helped Gwydion make a bride for Llew, who was his great-grandson.

Llew is identical with Lugh. Brought up under Gwydion's protection (who was his father), Llew was twice as big and twice as beautiful as any other youth his age. Llew's mother was Arianrhod, who wouldn't have anything to do with him because he was the cause of her altercations with Math. Arianrhod told Math she was a virgin, but when he tested her, she gave birth to two magical twin sons, Lleu Llaw Gyffes and Dylan Eil Ton.

Because of her anger, when Gwydion brought Llew to visit Arianrhod, she told him that the boy would never have a name unless she gave it to him. Gwydion was determined that the boy be named and so he tricked Arianrhod into giving the boy a name.

List of Celtic Gods and Goddesses

As you become more familar with Celtic mythology, you will see the interconnnections between Goddesses and Gods and their offspring. Following is a list of the Celtic Gods and Gods:

Abnoba Gaul Goddess of the hunt.

Adsagsona Celtic Goddess of the underworld and of magic.

Aengus mac Og (Angus, Angus Og, Oengus) Celtic God of love and beauty; Aengus is the healer of souls, associated with romance and courting. He is the son of the Dagda and Boann and husband to Caer, who was the daughter of the King of Connacht.

Aife (Aoife) A Scottish Queen whose rival was the Amazonian queen Scathach; consort of the sea god Manannan.

Aine Irish Earth and Sun Goddess of the summer solstice and Midsummer's Eve, with Finn as her consort; sorceress and Queen of the Faery, begotten by the spirits of fire and night; mate to Lugh.

Airmed A Goddess of witchcraft and herb lore.

Amaethon Agriculture and harvest God called the Harvest King; associated with the fruits of the harvest and the sickle, hoe, and plow.

Andraste Andrasta Fertility, war, and death Goddess associated with sanctuaries in sacred woods, like the one that existed on the Island of Mona (Anglesey).

Andraste (Britain) Warrior Goddess, the Goddess of victory.

Aobh Goddess of Ireland and wife of Llyr, the sea God.

Arawn Death, war, and ancestral God who was the King of Annwn, the Underworld; associated with the swine, magical beasts, the ancestral tree, water springs, shape-shifting, and the cauldron.

Ardwinna A Celtic Goddess of the forests and woods.

Arianrhod Stellar and lunar Goddess; daughter of Don (Dana); sister to Gwydion, Gobannon, and Amaethon; keeper of the "Silver Wheel" or "Silver Disc." Her palace is the Corona Borealis, which is called Caer Arianrhod (the Northern Crown).

Artio Celtic fertility Goddess of wildlife, who was portrayed in the form of a bear.

Badb (Badhbh, Badb Catha, Bav, Bov, Bodhbh) Druidess of the Tuatha De Danann and Goddess of war, inspiration, fury, and wisdom; known as the Battle Raven, with her name meaning "Scald-crow"; sister to Anu, Morrigu, and Mancha.

Banba Irish Earth Goddess representing the sacred land; part of the triad that included Folta and Eriu.

Bebhionn An Irish Underworld Goddess of pleasure.

Bel (Bilé, Eel, Belenus, Belenos) Sun God of light and healing, referred to as "The Shining One." His wife is the Goddess Belisama; associated with a golden harp, golden curved sword, a golden spear, and the sun disc; may also correspond to Bael, "The source of all light or life."

Belisama Associated with the rising Sun, a young Goddess of fire whose name means "like unto flame" and "the bright and shining one"; wife of Belenus.

Belisana Goddess of healing, laughter, and the forests; associated with the sun's warmth and woodland plants and animals.

Blodenwedd (Blodewedd, Blodeuedd) The most beautiful and treacherous Sun and Moon Goddess; called "White Flower" or "Flowerface"; associated with the white owl, the dawn, primroses, broom, cockle, oak, and meadowsweet.

Boann (Boi, Boanna) "She of the White Cow" and Mother of the herds, she is a fertility Goddess of the river Boyn, wife of the Dagda, and mother to Angus Og, Bridget, Bodb the Red, Mider, and Ogma.

Bodb Derg (Bodb the Red) The son of Dagda and Boann, Bard of the Tuatha De Danann, and King of the Sidhe.

Borvo (Bormo, Bormanus) Healing God of unseen and concealed truth and inspiration through dreams; Fire of water, the golden God, a Celtic Apollo, associated with hot springs, a flute, the sun disc, and a golden harp.

Bran (Bron) God of music and prophecy, protector of bards and poets; associated with singing, the Bard's harp, and the Sacred Head.

Branwen Welsh love Goddess called the White-Bosomed One and Venus of the Northern Sea. Her name means White Raven.

Bres God of fertility and agriculture and one of the first kings of the Tuatha De Danann.

Bridget (Bride, Brighid, Brigandu, Briget, Brede) Fertility Goddess of the Sacred Fire, the Sun, hearth, and home. Fire of fire, the bride Goddess of inspiration, poetry, medicine, healing, and smithcraft; daughter of Dagda and Boann, and wife to Bres; associated with the fire pot, Bridget's brass shoe, and the spindle and distaff.

Brigantia Celtic Briton Goddess of nature and the Sun; associated with the rivers, mountains, and valleys of the countryside.

Bronach An Irish Goddess of cliffs and precipices.

Caer An Irish swan maiden and wife to Angus.

Cailleach An ancient Goddess of the pre-Celtic peoples of Ireland, who controls the seasons and the weather; she was the Goddess of Earth, Sky, Moon, and Sun.

Camulus Celtic War God.

Carman A dark Goddess of destruction and ignorance. She had three sons: Dub (darkness), Dother (evil), and Dian (violence). The Tuatha De Danann, the deities ruled by the Goddess Danu, fought against Carman with their most powerful weapons. Finally, the sorceress Bechuille was able to undo Carman's curses.

Cilleac Bheur The Scottish Goddess of winter. Her staff can freeze the ground and wither the crops.

Cliodna Young aspect of the Dark Goddess; her name means "Shapely One"; bird Goddess and Faerie Queen associated with extraordinary beauty, shape-shifting, and apples; accompanied by three magical birds.

Concobar, mac Nessa "Concobar the son of the Black Queen";

also called Diamaide, "The Terrestrial God." He was the High King of Ulster and head of the Red Branch Heroes. His sister is Dechtere and Cu Chulain is his nephew.

Condatis British water God.

Cordemanon God of knowledge, ancestry, and travel; associated with the Great Book of Knowledge, stone circles, and sacred sites.

Coventina Goddess of the well and the womb of the Earth; associated with healing springs, sacred wells, childbirth, renewal, and the Earth.

Creiddylad (Creudylad) Daughter of the Sea god Llyr and a sea Queen, later known as the Welsh Goddess Cordelia in Shakespeare's play.

Creidne (Creidhne, Credne) Master sword maker named "The Bronze Worker"; associated with smiths, wrights, metal-working, and craftspersons.

Crom God of storms, lightning, and thunder.

Cu Chulainn The Hound of Culain, he was born with the strength of a man and a burning rage to conquer all in his path; champion of Erin. His consorts are the Goddesses Fand, Aifa, and Finnabair—and Emer, who was a mortal woman—and he is the son of Lugh and Dechtire. His story is found in "The Cattle Raid of Cu Chulainn."

Dagda (Dagda Mor, Eochaidh Ollathair, Ruadh Rofhessa) The "Good God" and "Good Hand"; chieftain Earth God of life, death, wisdom, prosperity, abundance, and knowledge; husband to Boann and consort to Ethniu, Ceara, and Morrigan. His daughters are Brigit, Ceacht, and Porsaibhean, and his sons are Angus Og, Bodb the Red, Mider, and Ogma; associated with oak trees, the flesh hook, a magical sword, the club, an inexhaustible cauldron, a magical harp, the chalice, and the rods of command; ruler of the bright half of the year. The King of Feasting, he has power over milk and corn, and possesses ever-laden fruit trees and two extraordinary swine: one that is always living, and one that is always cooking. He rules the seasons with the music from his harp.

Damona Goddess of fertility and healing; her name means "divine cow."

Dana (Danu, Dannu, Anu, Ana, Anna, Ann, Don) The Mother Goddess from whom the Tuatha De Danann were descended. Goddess of nature and consort of Bilé. Descended from Nemed, shape-shifter and Goddess of wisdom and creation. In stellar mythology, the constellation Cassiopeia honors the Goddess in its name, Llys Don, or "Danu's House."

Dechtere (Cechtire) She is referred to as a Goddess and sometimes as a mortal. She is the sister of Concobar mac Nessa and thus the daughter of the Black Queen (Nessa) and mother to Cu Chulain.

Deirdre "One who gives warning," or the older form Derdriu, "Oak prophet"; a humanized Goddess in the Red Branch tale of the Exile of the sons of Uisnach; the daughter of the God Morgan.

Dewi The Red Dragon God, which is the emblem of Wales.

Dia Griene The daughter of the Sun in ancient Scotland. She appears in a folk tale in which she is held captive in the Land of the Big Women. Dia Griene is then freed by the Cailleach, who is disguised as a fox. A young bumbler named Brian helps Cailleach free Dia Griene.

Dianacht "God of Curing or Swift in Power." Dianacht is the God of herbalism and healing; healing physician to the Gods; associated with the mortar and pestle. He is the father of Armedda and Miach, and grandfather to Lugh. He killed his own son.

Donn "The Brown or Dark One" is the God of the Dead. He dwells on the island Tech Duinn, "The house of Donn" off the southwest coast of Erin, and he bids his descendants welcome when they die. He is the chief son of Mil.

Dumiatis (Dumeatis) God of creative thought and teaching.

Dunus The God of mountains and fortifications.

Dwyn God of love and mischief.

Edain (Etain) Example of transmigration, heroine, Goddess of beauty and grace, and wife of King Mider; One of the "White Ladies" of the Faery.

Eithlenn (Ethniu, Ethna) She is the daughter of Baler of the evil eye, the consort of the Dagda, and the mother of Lugh.

Elayne (Elen, Elen Lwyddawg) Warrior Mother and Leader of the Hosts; powerful Goddess of Ireland, leadership and war.

Epona The horse Goddess; usually portrayed as riding a mare that is sometimes with a foal.

Eri (Irish) The mother of Bres.

Erie (Eriu) The Triple Mother Goddess of Erin, sometimes known as Ir, from which Ireland, the land of Ir, is derived; shape-shifter and Goddess of Sovereignty of the Land.

Esus Aspect of the Dark God; woodland God associated with hunting, the sword, the Golden Bull (Tarvos), and the bow and arrow; pictured as a woodcutter.

Fagus Monadic God of all beech trees.

Fal This God has a wheel of light, with which he can perform great magic, including flying through the air.

Fand Shape-shifter and Faery Queen of Ireland; daughter of the sea and wife to the sea God Manannan; ruler of the magical "Land Over Wave" and associated with the seagull.

Fen A war Goddess associated with Morrigan.

Fend The Sea Goddess and consort of Manannan mac Llyr.

Findabair Goddess of Connacht and the Otherworld, of beauty, grace, and love; daughter of Queen Medb of the Faery, who married a mortal man named Fraech.

Fliodhas Goddess of the woodlands; protector of animals and forests, associated with the doe.

Gabba (Gabis of the Abyss) Dark Queen and crone face of the Dark Mother; her name means "crystal."

Gobannon (Govannon, Goibniu, Goibhnie, Goibnll) The Divine Smith and God of magic, also called "Gobban the Wright" and Gobban Saer, "The Master Mason."

Grian Goddess of the Sun.

Gwalchmei God of love and music and son of the Goddess Mei; the "Hawk or Falcon of May."

Gwydion Shape-shifter and God of the arts, eloquence, kindness, and magic; son of Danu, nephew of Math, and brother of Ameathon, Gobannon, and Arianrhod. Gwydion gave his son

Llew his name and his right to bear arms and created Llew's bride for him.

Gwyn ap Nudd God of the Otherworld, the death chase, and the Wild Hunt.

Hellith God of the setting Sun and protector of souls of the dead.

Hertha (Herdda) Earth Goddess of rebirth and healing.

Kernunnos (Kairn, Kairnunos) Lord of the animals and God of life, death, wealth, and knowledge.

Kerridwen (Cerridwyn, Ceridwyn) The Goddess of knowledge and wisdom, who possessed the cauldron of inspiration.

Letha Midsummer harvest Goddess.

Llyr (Ler, Lir, Lear, Leer) Sea God of music and King of the oceans; husband to Aebh, and Aoife; father to Finonuala, Hugh, Fiachra, and Conn.

Luchta (Lucta, Luchtaine) Carpenter God and shield maker for the Tuatha De Danann.

Lugh (Lug, Lleu, Llew, Llaw Gyffes) Champion of the Tuatha De Danann, Sun God, and Master of all arts; God of poets, Bards, smiths, and war. Tailtiu was his foster mother. Lugh is the grandson of Diancecht and Baler of the Evil Eye. He is the son of Eithlenn (or Ethniu) and Dagda, consort to An, the Triple Goddess, and father of Cu Chulain.

Mabon (Mapon, Maponus) "The Divine Son" and "the Son of Light"; God of sex, love, magic, prophecy, and power.

Macha (MAha) A war Goddess and Druidess of the Tuatha De Danann. She may correspond to the Gaulish Epona—the horse Goddess of wisdom. Emhain Macha (EVan MAha), "The tracing of Macha," was named after her, as was Ard Macha, or Armagh as it's known today. She was invoked at Lughnassad. Macha has been Goddess/Consort during different incarnations to Nemhedh the Firbolg king, Cimbaeth, and the mortal Red Branch hero Crunnchu. Macha is associated with Morrigan.

Macha (Emhain Macha) Irish Queen and Threefold Sun Goddess of fertility, war, and ritual games; the "Sun Woman" and wife to Nemed and Nuada; ancestress of the Red Branch, daughter of Ernmas, and granddaughter of Net; associated with the horse, raven, and crow.

Manannan (Manannan ap Llyr, Manannan Mac Llyr) Shape-shifter; teacher; God of magic, the sea, and travel; consort to Rhiannon, consort to Fand, and son of Llyr. The Land of Promise, an Elysian island, is his home.

Math (son of Mathonwy) Seasonal King and Welsh God of magic, wisdom, enchantment, and sorcery; uncle and teacher to Gwydion; master Druid and teacher.

Medb (Maeve, Mab, Medhbh) "Intoxication or Mead." She is a Warrior Queen and Goddess of sex, fertility, and sovereignty. The pale-haired Medb was the Queen of Connacht and her Rath, or fort, was on the hill of Cruachain.

Mei (Mai, Meia) Mother of Gwalchmei and a solar and Earth Goddess.

Merlin (Myrddin) Woodland and nature God.

Mider (Midir) The Faery King, God of the Underworld, and consort to Etain; Bard and chess player; associated with the Isle of Man, the Faery hill of Bri Leith, the chess board, and game pieces; son of the Dagda and Boann, and brother to Angus, Bodb the Red, Lugh, Ogma. Mider's sister is Brigit. He is also the Sidhe Lord of Bri Leith.

Modrona (Modron, Madrona, Matrona) The Great Mother of Mabon (light).

Morgana The Death Mother and the Queen of Death, Goddess of fertility and war; daughter of Llyr (the sea) and Anuand (a shape-shifter).

Morrigan (Morrigana) "The Phantom Queen or Great Queen" and a sea Goddess, she is the triple Goddess of War, who shape-shifts into a raven. Her consorts are Dagda Mor and Nuada of the Silver Hand.

Morrigu The Dark Gray Lady and Queen of the Sea; Goddess of life, death, and magic.

Nantosuelta River Goddess whose consort is Sucellos.

Nemetona Protectress of the sacred Drynemeton, Warrior Goddess of the oak groves, and patron of thermal springs.

Nemon (Neman, Nemain) Daughter of Ernmas and sister to Macha, Goddess of War, whose name means "Venomous One" or "Frenzy."

Nessa "The Black Queen," who is the mother of Concobar and Dechtire, and the grandmother of Cu Chulain.

Nimue (Niniane, Niviene, Nymenche) Student and teacher to Merlin, her consort.

Nodens God of dreams and sleep.

Nuada (Lludd, Nudd, Lludd Llaw Ereint) The Good Father; first king of Tara; consort to Fea, the war Goddess, and to Morrigan; powerful chieftain God of thunder, kingship, rebirth, war, and wealth, who carries one of the Tuatha De Danann's four treasures: the sword from Findias.

Nwyvre God of space and the firmament, and consort to Arianrhod.

O Donoghlle The God of Lough Lean in Killarney, who visits the land of mortals at sunrise every Beltane.

Ogma (Ogmios) "The Binder," also called Trenfher, "Champion or Strong Man," and Grianainech, "Of the Sun-like Countenance." He is the God of eloquence, knowledge, and literature. Ogma invented the Ogham.

Pryderi Youthful shape-shifter God and son of the Goddess Rhiannon and the God Pwyll.

Pwyll Prince of Dyfed and King of the Otherworld. A pack of hounds accompanies him.

Rhiannon Queen Mother, Queen Mare, or the Great Queen, wife of Pwyll and Manannan.

Robur Forest King and Monadic Tree God of the forests, particularly oaks.

Rosemerta Goddess of abundance and plenty; wife to Lugh.

Sadv The ancient deer Goddess of the forests and nature; mother to Oisin, the poet.

Scathach (Scatbach) "The Shadowy One"; a war Goddess who ran a school for young heroes such as Cu Chulain.

Sinann (Sinand) The Goddess of the River Shannon. The White Trout and the Salmon of Knowledge are probably avatars or incarnations of Sinann. Her other names are: Cailb, Samuin (or Samain), Sesclend, Sodb, Saiglend, Samklocht, Gall, Cell, Dichoem, Dichuil, Dichuimne, Dichuinne, Dame, Darine, Der Uane, Egam, Agam, Gnim, Cluche, Cethardam, Nith Neuin,

Noenden, Badb, Blosc, Blear, Uaet, Mede, Mod—and she
recited this list in one breath.

Sirona Solar and astral Goddess; Borvo is her consort.

Smertullos The Preserver and Lord of Protection, God of the
abyss and the unmanifested.

Sucellos River God and twin to the Dagda, shape-shifter and God
of fertility and death.

Taillte Irish Earth Goddess and foster mother to Lugh.

Taliesin Son of Kerridwen; poet, prophet, and bard.

Taranis God of thunder, storms, and the seasonal cycle.

Tarvos Trigaranos God of vegetation and virility.

Tethra Sea God of magic.

Tlachtga The Matron Goddess of Tara.

Triana The Triple Goddess; Sun-Ana, Earth-Ana, and Moon-Ana;
Goddess of healing, knowledge, higher love, and wisdom.

Viviana (Vivian, Vivien) Goddess of love, birth, life, mothers,
childbirth, and children. Her consort is Merlin.

Gift From the Goddess Creative Visualization

This visualization is intended to help you connect with deity. It
is very powerful when tape-recorded and played back just
before going to sleep and upon waking. If you tape record this
visualization and want to use it before going to sleep, merely
alter the ending by saying, "I will now go to sleep and dream
peacefully and awaken feeling completely refreshed." You can
also alter the visualization, making it "Gift From the God Creative Visualization," by using the word "God" in place of "Goddess," and "he" instead of "her," and so forth, to coincide with
the gender change.

Begin by closing your eyes, breathing deeply, and relaxing.
Allow yourself to get as comfortable as you can. Breathe in to
the count of three, hold your breath for three counts, and then
exhale completely. Do this three times or more, deeply breathing in and out and relaxing more and more, allowing all of the

tensions, stress, and worries of the day to flow out of you every time you exhale. Each sound you hear in the room helps you to relax further and to become more peaceful.

Breathe white light into your body from all around you. Feel yourself breathing in the light through your skin, through the tips of your toes and the top of your head, softly and completely. As you breathe in the white light, feel it flowing through your body and warming you from your head to your toes.

Now very slowly visualize yourself walking down a garden path on a warm summer's day, the sun shining bright. The air is warm and a gentle breeze touches your face. You come to a garden gate. The gate is very ornate, and faces of animals and shapes of flowers and trees are fashioned in the intricate iron-work. Their eyes seem to come alive in the sunlight.

Slowly you open the gate, and as you do so, you notice the warmth of the metal on your hands. You walk unhurriedly through the gate into the garden, leaving the gate open behind you. As you enter through the threshold to the lush garden, the smell of roses, lavender, and jasmine fills your senses.

You can hear bees buzzing in the garden as you walk on, and the smell of water greets you as you approach a small pool of water fed by a natural spring. The spring bubbles softly over several large milky white quartz stones as it flows into the pool.

You sit down comfortably on the grassy bank next to the pool and look into the water. You can see the reflection of the trees circling the pool and yourself mirrored in the brightly lit water. You dip your hand into the water and feel the cool sensation, perhaps even drinking from the pool yourself.

Noticing some very small white quartz stones on the edge of the pool, you pick up three stones in your hand and begin to throw them into the pool, one at a time. Watch the ripples from each stone move outward and finally disappear before you toss in the next stone. With each stone you toss softly into the water, you feel more relaxed, peaceful, and warm.

Suddenly, you have the sensation and realization that you are not alone. As you look to your left, the image and form of the Goddess appears. Study her image for a few moments, using your breath to get an even clearer image of her. Taking a deep breath, you can see her clearly now. Communicate with her. If you know her name, call her by her name. If you don't know her name, ask her and she will tell you. Merge with her and become one with the Goddess. With each breath you take, her image becomes more defined and her face even more clear. She seems surrounded by a golden-white luminosity that spreads out from her being and melts into yours.

In her right hand, she holds a gift for you, perhaps a symbol, a flower, a sphere of light, a sensation, a name. Whatever the gift is, take it willingly and thank the Goddess. This gift is your divine gift.

In her left hand, she holds a stone. Notice what kind of stone it is and how it feels in your hand as you take it from the Lady. It may feel cool or hot, alive with energy or soothing and calm. These are magical gifts that you can use to communicate directly with the Goddess.

Now it is your turn to give the Goddess something in return, a song, perhaps, or a promise, whatever you choose. Give this gift to her now. Breathing slowly and completely, say whatever you need to say to her, silently. Visualize the experience even more clearly now, sensing every feeling and thought between you and the Goddess.

Suddenly, the Goddess stands up and beckons you to follow her. You carry your gifts with you as she leads you through the garden, showing you the many trees, plants, roses and other flowers, animals, and magical beings that live there. The bright sun shines upon everything—the leaves of the plants, the branches of the trees, and the path in front of you, lighting everything up with its pure rays. The Goddess reminds you that you can return to this magical garden whenever you choose, and then she takes your hand and guides you through the intricate iron gate, closing the gate behind you.

As you move through the gate, the Goddess becomes invisible, but she is still very much with you. You can sense her hand on yours. She is always with you. The gifts she has given you are eternal.

Slowly, you begin to move back into your body, remembering your gifts and what you have given the Goddess, knowing that these gifts are signs of your connection with the Goddess and the divine. Moving your hands, toes, and head, come back to the present moment completely, opening your eyes and breathing deeply.

Be sure to make a note of the gifts the Goddess gave you and what you gave her in return.

3

THE DRUIDS

Of Merlin wise I learned a song,—
Sing it low, or sing it loud,
It is mightier than the strong,
And punishes the proud.
I sing it to the surging crowd,—
Good men it will calm and cheer,
Bad men it will chain and cage.
In the heart of the music peals a strain
Which only angels hear;
Whether it waken joy or rage,
Hushed myriads hark in vain,
Yet they who hear it shed their age,
And take their youth again.

"Merlin's Song," by Ralph Waldo Emerson

The Origins of the Druids

The origins of the Druids emerge by our piecing together ancient history, folklore, and literary sources in Celtic and classical languages, combined with archaeological discoveries, literary and artistic works from the last few centuries, and the

70

current practices of modern Druids. The earliest recorded references to the Druids survive from the second century B.C., but these are in the form of third-hand quotations. Unfortunately, because of this much of the information on the Druids and their practices is speculative.

A great number of Irish epic texts speak of the Druids, but the literature and laws of Ireland were not written down until after Christianity swept through the Celtic countries. In *Celtic Bards, Celtic Druids,* R. J. Stewart points out, "None of the Celtic source literature is by druids." He adds, "In Ireland, the amount of poetic/druidic material in manuscripts, both translated and untranslated, is substantial . . . the bulk of the source material is unpublished, and still untranslated."

From what can be gleaned from the materials available, the Druids were an intellectual class or caste, dating from the most distant past of the Celts. In fact, some scholars propose that Druidism was the core of a great mystery tradition and held prior place in antiquity to all of the world's religions. Several Druidic principles mirror those in Buddhist, Hindu, and Jewish religions.

Most experts agree that the Druids stem from the Old Tribes of Europe. "The Welsh Triads" state that Druidism is the oldest religion in Britain. Others suggest the Druids may have migrated to the West from the Altai region in Siberia. Their mystical heritage may come from this remote area, known for its shamans and healers. It is probable that there was interaction and trade. Still other experts suggest the Druids originally came from Babylonia, Egypt, Tibet; were remnants of the Cult of the Dead; or were the descendents of Abraham of the Israelites. Theories of the origins of the Druids also encompass Atlantis, the fabled land that lies beyond the Pillars of Hercules.

The suggestion has been made that Egyptian ideology was brought to the West and into Druidism by Moses. Others suggest that Druids such as Abaris, a hyperborean Arch-Druid who visited Athens around 350 A.D., sought knowledge in foreign lands, sharing their teachings while gathering new ideas and practices along the way, much as spiritual leaders do today. Abaris rode on a golden arrow as Apollo's messenger and visited Pythagoras, who received and initiated him. Certainly, vast exchanges of goods and ideas occurred via the trade routes, not to mention through the Celts' invasion of other countries and cultures such as those of the Greeks and Italians. Some of these ideas were integrated and grafted onto the existing esoteric traditions.

Egyptians were early invaders of Europe, and evidence has been found that connects the Egyptians and Druids. The Egyptian Goddess Isis was venerated in northern Europe. The name of the city Paris stems from Barisis (Barque d'Isis), which translates as "the boat of Isis" and is depicted in the Coat of Arms of Paris as a "Sun Ship." The Egyptians referred to the Druids as the "People of the Sea."

Other early peoples who interacted with the pre-Celtic Druids were the Phoenicians, Babylonians, and Chaldeans. For example, some of the deities of the ancient Britons are similar or the same as those of the Phoenicians, such as the Sun God Bel. And as mentioned in chapter 1, all of the successive waves of peoples who invaded Ireland also impacted Druidic tradition: the Cessair, Partholon, Nemed, Fir Bolg, Tuatha De Danann, and Sons of Mil Espane.

Druidic tradition is closely akin to ancient Indo-European traditions, such as the shamans of Eastern Europe, as previously noted, and also the Brahmins of India. Accordingly, the Celts and Hindus have common ancestors in the race called the Battle-Axe People. This race lived in southern Russia and their mark was a perforated stone battle-axe. Most scholars agree that the Indo-European language spoken by the Celts derived from the same source as Sanskrit, which was the classical language of the Hindus. It may well be that in pre-Christian times, the ancient mysteries were more akin to one another than was previously considered. Many similarities exist between the Celtic and Indian deities, an example being that the Druids were the priest-astronomers of Europe and the Indian Brahmins were the priest-astronomers of the East.

Historical evidence indicates the existence of Druids in Ireland, Britain, and throughout Gaul (mainland Europe), including Spain, Italy, Galatia, and the Danube Valley, and other adjacent areas influenced by the Celts. Druids often traveled and met together, which created a sense of unity among the Celtic peoples across Europe.

Some suggest that Druidism originated with the builders of the megaliths, a pre-Celtic pagan people who lived in northern and western Europe prior to 2000 B.C. Even if the Druids did not stem from the pre-Celtic megalith builders, the Druid astronomer-priests were their leaders. The Druids wisely integrated the folk traditions, superstitions, and festivals of these pre-Celtic peoples into their own practices and philosophy.

Regardless of their origin, the Druids, their beliefs, and their practices were greatly influenced by a diverse array of ancient cultures and Eastern traditions, including the mysterious Anunnaki, the ancient Sumerians, Egyptians, and the Hindus, as well as the mysterious Hyperboreans of the Northern Isles, the Pythian oracles of Greece, and the Celts. The Druids had an ancient kinship with the Greeks, and Druidic spiritual beliefs and practices were referred to by Aristotle. In Homer's time, the Druids' power and influence extended as far as Poland in Eastern Europe. Also, remember that the Celts invaded Greece and sacked Delphi around 280 B.C., integrating Greek philosophy and ideas into their own.

By the time the Druids came to the British Isles, they were a well-organized order with a fully developed knowledge of the arts and sciences. They were most likely a surviving priesthood who followed the Old Religion of Europe, who came to the

Mediterranean from such areas as Brittany (France) and Spain, and who settled in southern England. By blending Neolithic Mediterranean culture with the beliefs of the native peoples of early Britain, the Druids became a very effective and cohesive governing body.

The Druids honored and worshiped the sun, utilizing such solar observatories as Stonehenge in Britain. Their Goddesses and Gods were the fabled Tuatha De Danann (refer to chapter 2). These personified deities were the guardians of social law and the keepers of the ancient wisdom. The Druids looked upon deity as ancestral rather than creational.

The king and his Druid formed an essential couple, with the Druid being the more powerful of the two. The Druid always spoke before the leader in assembly, and often a king or queen was a leader of his or her people only because the Druids decreed it to be so. For example, King Arthur became king only after Merlin orchestrated everything so that Arthur could be recognized as king. Temporal power bowed to spiritual power.

From the stories and texts, it becomes obvious that the Druids were the sovereign power in all of Celtica, religiously, socially, and politically. They declared war or made peace and had the authority as international judges to the point where they could go onto a battlefield, stand between the two opposing forces, and stop them from fighting. Celtic texts also mention that Druids had their own small armies and that every Druid traveled with a group of bodyguards. Druids, unlike most of the Celts, were not necessarily tied to tribal locations and allegiances.

The Druids knew how to read the celestial patterns. Their ability to gauge the seasonal cycles and weather changes gave them the cutting edge in the agrarian and herding Celtic soci- Druids also possessed a body of teachings of a scientific ut natural phenomena and universal laws, which v was also extremely useful on a day-to-day basis.

The Greek writers were the first to record the word *Druidae*. Several interpretations of the etymology of the word *Druid* appear throughout literature. Pliny the Elder suggested *Druid* was cognate with the Greek *drus* ("drys, dhrys") meaning an oak, with a reference to the same on a fifth century B.C. lead tablet found in the Zeus sanctuary at Dodona. Other scholars imply that *Druid* stems from the Old Celtic name for an oak, which is *derw*. Certainly, the oak tree and thunder were both key symbols and elements in Druidism. Still other interpretations include *dru-wid* or *dru-vid*, meaning "oak knowledge," with *wid* or *vid* meaning "to know" or "to see." Others propose that the word *Druid* is from the British *dar*, signifying superior, or *Gwydd*, meaning "a priest" or "wise one." In Scottish Gaelic, *Druidh* means "a magician or sorcerer," and the word *drud* in Old English indicates a discreet, wise, or learned person.

The Druids became an integral part of Celtic culture, and the Celts integrated and continued the Druidic tradition. Even though Druidism was diverse, with somewhat different regional variations, it embraced Celtic spirituality, and at the peak of its power and influence controlled many aspects of the Celts' civic and religious lives.

The Druids worshiped the Tuatha De Danann, who were the fabled Hyperboreans as previously mentioned in chapter 2. The Hyperboreans resided on the islands at the northernmost reaches of civilization, beyond the North Wind, known for practicing Druidism, sorcery, shape-shifting, and astronomy.

Some scholars postulate that Celtic Druidism in Ireland reached its peak long before that of the rest of Britain and Gaul and that originally it was from Ireland where the British and Gallic Druids gathered their teaching and wisdom. Also, Ireland has what is considered a more pure strain of Druidism because the Romans did not invade the country.

Druid practices and philosophy traveled with the Celtic people as they populated Gaul, northern Italy, the Iberian

Peninsula, and Asia Minor, as well as the Balkans, Britain, Wales, Scotland, and Ireland. At the height of their power, Celtic culture and the influence of the Druids spread from the British Isles to Turkey.

One of the first references to Druidism in Ireland is of Drostan, a Druid of the Irish Picts, who designed a magic bath of milk that healed the war-wounded. The Druid of Criomhthan, Chief of Leinster, made a similar bath. The Irish-Pictish Druids were driven into Scotland and many magical traditions in Scotland stemmed from them. Practices and stories have been handed down from generation to generation via the lineages of bards in Wales, Brittany, and Scotland, and by the Irish poets, which is proof of the survival of the living Druid tradition.

The Druids are part of every Celt's heritage. They are seen today as the end product of a long story: a story that shows how a recurrent pattern of thought, experience, and emotion about some of humankind's eternal problems can persist and be the fodder for thinkers from Hesiod in Greece of the eighth century B.C. to modern times. Before the Roman invasion, the Druids and their beliefs and practices flourished, free from outside influences.

Unfortunately, much of the information written down about the Druids comes from the Romans, particularly Julius Caesar, who emphasized and embellished the so-called savagery and brutality of the Druids as a way to discredit and place them in an unfavorable light. Most of it was pure propaganda. Claiming the Druids sacrificed people was all part of the Roman campaign against the Druids. Caesar's unapproved invasion into Celtic Gaul was only later given sanction by the state after he was successful. (Remember that the Celts, in 387 B.C., invaded Rome and held it for seven months, leaving only after being debilitated by an epidemic and exacting a large sum from the Romans.)

After the Roman invasion, the Romans focused a great deal of energy on eradicating all signs of the Druids, including the systematic extermination of the Druids and their practices. Caesar ordered massacres, and the Roman soldiers killed Druid men and women on sight and persecuted them to the point of driving them underground in Europe. The practices and philosophy of the Druid order were an extreme threat to the Roman way of life, especially the idea of giving women equal rights and status.

Formally, the Druids ceased to exist around the fourth century A.D. Even so, Druid traditions and practices were kept alive through the oral traditions passed down through the centuries, especially in Ireland, Wales, and Scotland. To some extent, Scottish witchcraft stems from Celtic Druidism, with similar religious and magical practices. Often, women were the conservators of the Druid mysteries, and evidence shows that female Druids certainly existed.

Druidism represented an element of rugged individualism and resistance to the Romans in Gaul and Britain. Hailed as an enemy philosophy and persecuted in Gaul, with Roman campaigns against Druid sanctuaries in Britain and by degradation in Ireland, Druidism was an element of resistance because it fostered cohesiveness. In this way, Druidism transcended both geographic boundaries and clan or tribal connections. The Druids became the priests of the Celtic Christian Church during the Roman occupation of Britain from approximately 100 to 400 A.D. These Druid priests were later transformed into the Christian Saints.

Druid Philosophy

Druidism is primarily a philosophy or spirituality that emerged from the pre-Celtic and Celtic religions. It lacks the dogmatic signature of most religions, which is important to keep in mind when discussing Druidism. Celtic spirituality relied entirely on Druidism, mixing the local Gods and Goddesses, heroes and heroines, together with traditional Druidic philosophy. The Celtic Druids communed with the Gods and Goddesses, without themselves adopting divine authority.

The Druidic philosophy embodied all aspects of universal awareness (body, mind, and spirit). R. J. Stewart, in his book *Celtic Druids, Celtic Bards,* writes:

> Druidism might be likened to a "New Religious Philosophy" of the Celts, a set of dominant, highly refined beliefs and practices that was the culmination of wisdom and experience laid down over thousands of years by the Celts and pre-Celtic peoples of Europe.

Druidism was not a single esoteric tradition, but a holism of many philosophies and religions.

In all Celtic languages today, the word *philosopher* means "person of wisdom." The Welsh *Athroniaeth* is based on *athro* meaning "teacher." In *The Druids,* Peter Ellis notes:

> But perhaps more interesting is the fact that in Old Irish are found other words for philosopher; "cailleoir," whose basis means auguring or star divination and which is used in Gaelic in the form "caileadar" to mean philosopher or star-gazer; while a further Old Irish term, "feallsamhacht," survives in Manx as "fallosgyssahgh," which means astrologer.

Druids were associated with prophecy, judgment, truth, and virtue, and had a long established reputation as philosophers outside the Celtic world. The Druid order attended and advised chieftains, kings, queens, and other leaders who were responsible for the land, tribes, and clans. They keenly understood the need for certain strongholds throughout the Celtic countries, establishing colleges and educating students from the many

Celtic lands. For example, Northwest Wales, because of its close proximity to the sea and trade routes, was a focal point and center for the Druids, particularly the Druid college at Anglesey. Besides being a major port of sea, Anglesey (the Isle of Mona) was also a watchtower between Wales, Ireland, and Scotland.

A Greek writer in the third century A.D., Diogenes Laertius, noted that there were three philosophical Druidic ideals: to revere Divine Being, to live with courage, and to abstain from harmful actions. In his writing he also quotes Aristotle (384–322 B.C.) and Sotion of Alexandria (200–170 B.C.) on the Druids, which implies that their order was active and influential at that time.

Dualism of good and evil did not exist in Celtic Druidic philosophy. There was nothing fearful about life for the Druids, primarily because they had a deep understanding of spiritual energies. The Druids were spirituality conscious and connected. They were not seekers of heroic death or annilation like the Hindus or Egyptians. Instead, they were concerned with mirroring metaphysical ideals and the wisdom of nature in the social structure. They felt that there was a deeper reality beyond appearance.

This deeper reality is what the Druids called the Truth. To the Druids, Truth was the Word and was sacred. There was magic and power in words and often the very act of Truth had magical power. The Old Irish word for truth is linked with holiness, faithfulness, and justice. To the Druids, the truth was the highest power and the sustaining force in creation. The word, or truth, was the ultimate cause of all being in the universe.

Metaphysical concerns and quests into dimensional space always excited the Celtic Druids. This was exemplified in the Druidic architecture, which could be perceived as Celtic *feng shui*. The spirits, energies, terrain, and orientation were all considered in the structure and placement of dwellings.

The Druids had a sacred and spiritual connection with the

land and with the landscape, which mirrored and held safe the spirits (sleeping or active) of the Goddess and God. There are numerous stories about how valleys, mountains, hills, and other natural features of the countryside got their names. Interestingly, one of the most positive things that has come out of the modern Druid traditions and practices is this reclaiming of our connection and active relationship with the sacred land, the Earth.

The Druids considered the physical, Earthly dimension as only one of the several dimensions a person could experience. This view of reality is repeatedly woven through Celtic myths and stories. This expanded view of what constitutes reality formed the core of Druidic philosophy, spirituality, and magic.

The mysterious connecting thread that wove the human (physical) world to the divine world and the Otherworlds was called "Nwywre," which is also the name of the Celtic God of the Firmament. Nwywre is symbolized by the serpent and is considered the creative power of the Earth, the ether, light, and energies that linked the mortal with the divine. This serpent energy is constantly moving and changing. The union of Nwywre and the other elements of the universe created life and spirit.

For the Druids, spirit resided in the head. One of the Bardic themes that goes back to Druid magic is that of the sacred prophetic head. The severed head is found in many Irish stories, for example, the story of Bran the Blessed. The head is a bridge between the mortal and the Otherworld, where divine and human perception become one.

Bran is the king of the Isle of the Mighty (Britain). He gives Branwen, his sister, as wife to Matholwch and gives Matholwch the magic cauldron as a token of peace for insults by Bran's brother Efnissien to Matholwch. He then has to rescue Branen from her servitude in the Irish kitchen by wading across Irish sea with the British fleet. Bran defeats the Irish, who

offer to make Gwern, Branwen's son, king. At the feast to cele-
brate Gwern's accession, Efnissien throws Gwern into the fire
and kills him. Hostilities continue. Bran is mortally wounded in
the heel and asks that his head be cut off and buried at the
White Tower of London. The head of Bran continues convers-
ing as his friends do as he asks. Tradition says that his head was
buried under the White Hill to protect the country, but King
Arthur dug it up, as he wanted to be the sole guardian of
Britain.

The Druids felt that you could live on the Earth, the Otherworld, or elsewhere, and be reincarnated again and again. There
existed a constant exchange of souls between what could be
considered parallel worlds. Upon death in the mortal world, the
soul traveled to the Otherworld. Upon death in the Otherworld,
the soul was reborn into the mortal world. The Druids acted as
middlemen and middlewomen between the mortal and Otherworlds. They could see into, move about in, and freely traverse
the thread from one world to another. The believed that life in
both worlds was essentially the same.

Death was seen as the middle of a long life, as the Druids
believed in the immortality of the soul, conceived and empow-
ered by an indestructible universal divinity. They asserted that
the soul and the universe were indestructible, but at some time,
fire and water would prevail.

Druid Colleges

As the intellectual class, the Druids focused on knowledge, both
esoteric and exoteric. They held the body of the land and
people in their power and were the reservoir of Celtic knowledge, which included much from other civilizations such as the
Egyptians, Greeks, and Phoenicians. Controlling the Celtic education, the Druid caste thus wielded incredible influence.

Along with spiritual sanctuaries in forests and caves that the

Druids were known to frequent, they had colleges throughout Celtic countries. There they imparted the Druidic body of knowledge, training students for positions of power and leadership—to be philosophers, historians, seers, priests and priestesses, teachers, administrators, chieftains, officials, and doctors, as well as scientists, astrologers, Bards, judges, law makers, astronomers, and diviners.

The Druids of Gaul would go to Britain to visit famous schools and sanctuaries. British Druidism had an equally high reputation in Ireland, and the Irish Druids went to Britain to complete their education. Some students of Druidism attended colleges because of lineage, while others were admitted for training in many valuable occupations. The sons of Gaulish chiefs were sent to these Druidic colleges for instruction, and Gaulish physicians trained by the Druids were preeminent until the Roman proscription. Legend has it that a great Druidic school called "Mur Ollamhan" (the City of the Learned) existed in 927 B.C., and many references to such schools appear in Irish mythology. For instance, Cuchulainn studied under Cathbad the Druid at a Druidic school.

Druidic knowledge and philosophy was developed and taught by specifically trained priests and priestesses, but as mentioned previously, science and spirit were blended together, making the Druids more priest(ess)-scientists. These priests and priestesses merged several functions together. The Druidic colleges were interdisciplinary, in which esoteric and exoteric areas of study were not considered separate, but connected together into a greater whole. For example, astronomy and astrology were taught as one and formed a primary theme in Druidism. Druids knew the size and shape of the Earth, which in that era, was unfathomable. Concepts such as free will and fair play were also taught. Everything was woven together into one, especially knowledge and wisdom.

Druidic students studied a prescribed body of knowledge at

Druidic colleges. Most scholars agree that any acolyte wanting to train for the priesthood studied a period of nineteen to twenty years, which is one complete "great year" cycle. Some suggest it may be that the period of Druidic study lasted until the person was nineteen or twenty years old.

A Druid's course of study included genealogy, history, geography, and geometry, as well as architecture, healing, astrology, and astronomy. Students would specialize in skills such as astronomy, astrology, divination, music, musical composition, singing, poetry, medicine, genealogy, history, meteorology, philosophy, teaching, prophecy, prose writing, agriculture, animal husbandry, science, geography, law, or languages.

Students were required to have formidable memories and memorized vast genealogies for the scattered Celtic tribes. Memorizing genealogies and histories in the form of poems and epics was not done merely to keep track of lineages, but the poems and epics were also a record of the history of humankind as well as the keys to magical practices and ancestral power.

The Druids used riddles and puns as ways of teaching. For example, in the story "The Wooding of Ailbe," riddles such as these appear: What is whiter than snow? (The Truth); What is blacker than the raven? (Death); What is swifter than the wind? (Thought).

There has always been a strong connection between the Druids and the poetic, prophetic, and artistic crafts. The creative and intuitive arts were preserved and disseminated by the Druids and were imparted to their acolytes. Much of the time was spent learning and doing ritual magic, prophecy, and visionary work.

The Druids taught natural philosophy and the nature of the Gods and Goddesses, about the world and the size of lands, as well as the stars and their motions. For example, Pollux was the Druidic star associated with immortality of the soul and Procyon was the star of healing. Spica was the Druidic star linked with riches and fame, while Vega was the star that controlled the seas. Altair was connected with the soul of King Arthur and Rigel was associated with Cuchulain, as was Bellatrix. The Druids taught that the Milky Way was a bridge to the stars and to the Otherworld. The Pleiades were important to the Druids as this constellation rose and set in November and May, marking important seasonal cycles. They revered the "Watcher," or royal stars, which signaled the seasonal changes, associating them with the Old Ones, who were the ancient Gods who guarded the entrance to the Otherworld.

The rights of women in Celtic culture far exceeded those of women in Rome or Greece, and Celtic women were noted for their courage and skill in battle. Celtic Druids included women in their political and spiritual life while the Romans viewed women as inferior pleasure objects and a means of perpetuating the race. Numerous Celtic women are found as warriors and figures of supreme authority, for example, Queen Boudiccea and Queen Medb of Connacht. In Britain, there was no objection to being led by women and there was no rule to exclude women from commanding armies or keeping the female line from the throne. The old Celtic heroes are always referred to as being the sons of a particular mother, which implies that matrilinear succession was alive and well at one time in Celtic history. The northern British Celtic tribes called the Picts had a matrilineal succession of kingship.

Women were venerated as instruments of the Goddess. Goddess energy is erotic, and one of women's roles in the Druid priest(ess)hood, for instance, was an ancient one, that of the sexual and fertile Goddess. Celtic culture was more open in its attitudes toward sexual relationships. Several scholars suggest that a form of Western Tantric yoga, which originated in Egypt and Greece, was practiced by both female and male Druids. In all probability, the Druids were well aware of the power and uses of Tantra and sex magic, by whatever name these practices were referred to at that time. Strabo also connected the Druidesses with the priestesses of Bacchus (Dionysus). Examples are the Druid Merlin's two female students, Nimue and Viviana, who remain to this day living symbols of witches and sleepers. I doubt very much whether Merlin and his female apprentices were spending all of their time up in Merlin's tower making potions. In fact, Nimue has been described in literature as the daughter of Dinas (a thinly disguised Dionysus). She says openly that Merlin is her thought and her desire, and without him, she has neither joy nor wealth. In Merlin she has set all of her hope, and she abides no other joy but of him.

The psychosensory transmittal of knowledge through sexual experience was a natural part of Celtic Druid tradition, and much has been lost as this method of learning has all but disappeared or been corrupted in contemporary culture. Jean Markale, in his book *Merlin: Priest of Nature,* explains:

> In the Celtic tradition, as elsewhere in numerous "archaic" civilizations, the initiation into knowledge does not take place without specific sexual relations between master and discipline. One could say that knowledge is transmitted as much by the psychosensory activity awakened by sex as by reasoned intelligence.

With the advent of Christianity, sexual psychosensory transmittal was unfortunately discarded, and the link between body and spirit severed.

Women were also trained at the Druidic colleges as lawyers, leaders, teachers, judges, and priestesses, among other professions. Druid women seers were called by names such as Druidess, Dryad, priestess, and prophetess. The Christian scribes later transformed and transcribed the Druidesses into sorceresses and witches.

The colleges and sacred groves of the Druids were destroyed by the Romans in 60 A.D. Tactius describes the Roman soldiers killing the inhabitants at the Druid college at Anglesey in North Wales, which was the very center of Druidism. The Romans systematically destroyed all of the colleges, groves, libraries, and artifacts, often building over sacred sites as a means of eradicating the Druidic influence. After the Roman invasion, the Druid colleges were turned into monasteries. The Druid caste continued its teaching, but instead of holding classes in colleges, they instructed their students in caves, forests, and remote valleys. Some say that to this day there still exists the unbroken survival of the teachings of the Druidic colleges.

Druids, Vates, and Bards

The intellectual classes of Gaul (mainland Europe) were divided into three: Druids, Vates, and Bards. In Ireland the same classes were known as Drui, Bard, and Fili. Modern Druidism still has the three priest(ess)hoods of Druid, Vates, and Bard. To be a Druid, a person gathered knowledge of many arts and skills. Students went through the training in all three orders. In Welsh Druidism, the Druids are the officials, judges, and law givers. Two ways they enforced their judgments and laws were the *geis* (*geasa*), which was a taboo or prohibition, and the *glam dicin,* which was a satirical incantation or curse directed against a specific person. In *The Druids,* Peter Ellis observes:

> Druids could pronounce the "glam dicin" or the "geis" to assert their authority. The "geis" was primarily a prohibition placed on a particular person and since it influenced the whole fate of that person, it was not imposed lightly. Anyone transgressing a "geis" was exposed to the rejection of his (her) society and placed outside the social order.

The *troscad,* or ritual fast, was also a legal way to settle grievances and compel justice. The Druids could fast against a king, people could fast against their leader.

The Bards preserved and created the oral poetic wisdom, while the Vates were the healers, diviners, and prophets. The Bardic candidate proceeded up through the various degrees: Mabinog (which is a pupil or apprentice), Filidh, Brehon, Gwyddon, Derwydd, and finally Penderwydd (the chief of song). There was also a Penderwydd who was the chief of chiefs called the Phantarch. This person was chosen to rule over the Bardship of old Albion. Folklore says that the Island of the Mighty was protected by the Phantarch as if he was standing underneath it and supporting it on his own shoulders.

Bards were poets, musicians, singers, and storytellers. For example, Taliesin was a Bard who recited and told of the universal wisdom of the three worlds: the Overworld, the Middle World (planetary life), and the Underworld. These three things make a Bard: playing the harp, knowing the ancient lore, and having poetic power. In *Celtic Druids, Celtic Bards,* Robin Williamson writes:

> The Gaelic word for poem or song is "dan," which really means not only song but skill and destiny. It includes the notions of praising and foretelling, and more importantly, magical power over the article or person so treated.

The Bards knew of the invisible power of language and how the spoken word could empower or destroy, depending upon the intention and intonation of the orator. They always maintained that their language stemmed from a source in the Otherworld. It was a poetic, imaginative language filled with rhythm and cadence, a language alive with meaning that was a combination of mist and starlight and spoke to the soul. The Bards knew that poetry was not merely words, but the stones in a river, a lover's caress, the waves of the sea, a tear in a child's eye, and the spirits of the land. On the lips of a Bard, a story or poem became a kind of prayer or history, an amazing revelation, in which poetry and song are creations of almost paralyzing beauty.

The Bardic schools were active until the seventeenth century A.D., and were a continuation of the Druidic schools. Courses in mystical incantation, poetic methods for divination, and learning how to satirize and punish wrongdoers were included.

The Vates were the healers of the Druid order. The Druid healers knew the properties and uses of herbs, trees, and minerals. They knew how to set bones and stitch up wounds, but healing also involved invoking the Goddess and God, working with subtle life energies, and communicating with the spirit world, including ancestral spirits.

The Vates of the Gauls of Italy were similar to the Druids and organized in a like manner. A comparative study of the Druidic order shows that it was definitely pan-Celtic and an essential part of the organization and core structure of Celtic society. The Druid order succeeded in uniting the many scattered Celtic tribes into a cohesive group through similarity of beliefs and laws.

Even after Christianity swept across the Celtic lands, there remained close associations between the Druids and Celtic Christianity. The Bards (filids) were basically Christianized Druids, but it was through them that the legends, myths, stories, and religious practices were carried on. Much Druidic lore has survived in Ireland as the Brehon Law. Also many Celtic saints are the Druids of old or are variations of the ancient Tuatha De Danann, such as St. Anne with Anu and St. Bridget with Bridget.

Druid Practices and Rituals

Most people think of the Druids as white-robed folks engaged in unusual ceremonies and rituals at Stonehenge at Midsummer. This is more a product of Pliny's Roman imagination and modern fantasy. A Druid's garb would have more likely been a multi-colored cloak fastened with a gold broach and a headdress of antlers or a ceremonial hat or totemic mask. A Celtic chieftan, uncovered in 1968 in Southern Germany, was buried wearing silk embroidered robes; a gold-banded, wide leather belt; a gold bracelet and dagger; gold broaches on his cloak; and a birch bark hat.

Druidic practices and rituals were orally communicated only to the initiated, the most illustrious practices being magic, shape-shifting, divination, and prophecy. Initiates into the ranks of the Druids underwent a "purification in the cauldron" called the cauldron of inspiration, which was a ritual where they traveled to the Otherworld and then returned.

Druidism became synonymous with "magic" as the words *magus* and *magic* were used in place of *Druid*. All religious ceremonies and festivals were regulated by the Druids. For example, the Druids practiced a form of baptism called *baisteadh geinntlidhe,* meaning "the rain wedge of protection." The Druids used water to symbolically purify, baptizing children and singing rituals over the newborns. The Druidic baptism of the Welsh Gwri of the Golden Hair shows that the practice was not confined to Ireland.

Druids also conducted funerary rituals for the departed. They celebrated the rebirth of the soul in the Otherworld with a feast, funeral games, and a wake. The body was covered by green birch tree branches and then brought to the grave. The Druids then chanted a ritual over the body and delivered a funeral oration.

Like other ancient priest(ess)hoods, they studied the movement of the Sun, Moon, and stars. Lunar days singled out by the Druids were: (1) the day of the new Moon, (2) the sixth day of the Moon, and (3) the day of the full Moon. The Druids were primarily Sun worshipers and the ancient British custom of lighting bonfires at certain times of the year is of Druidic origin

and has continued into modern times. Fire is still carried
deiseal, or clockwise, around people, animals, crops, and houses
for protection and fruitfulness. The Celtic fishermen still begin
their journey by rowing or steering their boats sunwise, keeping
with the natural order of the universe.

The tradition of lighting a fire is a ritual proclamation of
ascendancy by the one who lights it, which means that the
person who actually lights the fire is declaring his or her position of power, for example, king or chief. This is described in
several Celtic stories. At some of the solar festivals, the Druids
practiced fire walking, using a special ointment on the soles of
their feet. Fire walking was thought to be as stimulating as
drugs in activating visions and prophecy.

Celtic magic is an ancient practice firmly rooted in the Celtic
pantheon, in nature, and in the elements. Druids harnessed the
forces of nature and could cause dense fog, destructive storms,
and snow, or dry up the wells. Celtic stories and folk tales
reflect the magic that was practiced by the Druids and Celts.
The writers of antiquity often cite the native proclivity of the
Celtic mind for prophecy and magic. The Irish series of sagas
are unmatched among the world's mythologies for their magical
qualities.

The ancient world was as deeply impressed by the philosophies, teachings, and mysteries of the Druids as it was by those
of Egypt or Chaldea. There is a great deal of trustworthy evidence that a complete system of magic, associated with a definite body of mystical knowledge and arcane thought, was
practiced by the Druids of ancient Britain and Ireland.

Pliny remarks that it seems possible that the Druids taught
magic to the Persians. Diodorus Siculus, Timagenes, Hippoly-
tus, and Clement of Alexandria all believed that Pythagoras
had received his mystical philosophy from the Celtic Druidic
priests of Gaul. In fact, the Druids used ciphers and numbers
according to the Pythagorean skill to foretell the future.

Valerius Maximus said that to jeer at the notions of the Druids' doctrine of immortality would also be to laugh at the notions of Pythagoras.

Almost every page of early Irish literature has a reference to the Druids' magical power. Ellis observes, "The common name for magician in Ireland was 'corrguinech' and his art, magic or sorcery, was 'corrguine.' In the story of the Battle of Magh Tuireadh, the 'corrguinech' cast his spell standing on one foot, with one arm outstretched and with one eye closed and uttered the 'glam dichenn' curse, to inflict injury on his enemies." Lugh and Cuchulainn also used the same one foot, one hand, one eye ritual in battle.

Magical potions made by the Druids were also considered extremely valuable. The *nawglan,* or "the sacred nine," was a specially prepared mixture the Druids and bards used in rituals to walk between worlds or to enter the spirit world. It was made from the ashes of the nine sacred woods: willows of the streams, hazel of the rocks, alder of the marches, birch of the waterfalls, ash of the shadows, yew of the plain, elm of the glens, rowan of the mountains, and oak of the sun.

Magical tools such as staffs made of yew, hawthorn, or rowan wood were used by Druids. Magical rods and wands were also used, were often made of yew, and were a symbol of position and stature. One story mentions that after Llyr's two wives died, he married once again. His third wife, Aoife, was so jealous of Llyr's children that she changed them into swans by touching them with her Druidic wand. The rod of a Druid, *slat an draoichta,* was a branch adorned with small hanging bells. Mannanan Mac Llyr had a magical apple branch with silver bells.

Druidism is based on working with the energies of the universe. Druids practiced astrology and the Druidic zodiac is older than the Graeco-Roman zodiac. Personal horoscopes were drawn up by astrologer Druids, such as the Irish Druid Cathbad, who drew up Deirdre's horoscope.

The Druids embraced the concepts of reincarnation and transmigration and were master shape-shifters, changing into animal forms such as an eagle or deer. Shape-shifting exists in folklore around the world and was one of the practices of the Druids. The ancient Druids used the magic power of *faet fiada* to become invisible. *Faet fiada* literally means "the appearance of a wild animal."

The Druids acted as the diviners and augurs of the Celtic people. The Celtic Druids excelled above all others in the skill of augury and divination, and these practices constituted a mainstay of Celtic society. The Druids used certain gemstones and crystals, such as crystal balls, for divination. One such crystal ball, two and a half inches in diameter, surmounts the Scottish scepter. The Druid's or serpent's eggs may have been forms of quartz crystal. The *glain-nan-Druidhe,* or Druid's crystal, is well known in Scotland, and in Wales and Ireland small green or blue crystals (sometimes streaked with blue, white, and red) are mentioned as Druid Glass in texts such as *Britannia* by William Camden.

Another practice of the Druids was divining living things in nature such as the shapes of clouds, tree roots, or birds. Bird augury was a particular specialty of the Druids. They would watch the flight patterns, number, direction, season, and time of day of bird sightings, discerning specific future events from the information. One of the birds the Druids paid close attention to was the wren. They thought the wren to be supreme among all birds, and considered the Druid King of the Birds sacred to the Bard Taliesin. The wren's chirping was used as an augury, and the direction and proximity of its call were highly significant.

Famous as seers and renowned for their divination skills and the accuracy of their prophecies, the Druids impressed the ancient world with their power as prophets. Merlin is probably the most well-known Druid prophet. His prophecies cover the end of humankind and the unraveling of the universe.

Prophecy was a clearly defined function primarily reserved for the Vates, one of the three degrees of the Druid order, the other two being Druids and Bards, as previously discussed. Often, the circumstances of the hero's death had been foretold by Druid seers. For example, a Druidess told Severus Alexander that he should go to war, but to beware of his soldiers. During the campaign, Severus was assassinated by his own men. Another example was the Druid God King Balor who was told by a Druid that his grandson would kill him. Ethnea, Balor's only child, was shut in a tower to prevent this from happening, but still, she had three sons. Balor killed two of them, but the one who escaped, Lugh, returned to fulfill the Druid prophecy.

Druids and the Sacred Grove

The dryads, or tree spirits, according to Druidic belief, came to Earth, dancing on the first rays of the Sun, many moons before humankind appeared. Described as the first spiritual link with the cosmos, the dryads were conceived during the lunar eclipses at the time of the Full Moon and came down to Earth at the winter solstice at the beginning of time as deities or incomprehensible spirits that had previously been hidden or concealed. In this light, it is important to remember that in Celtic languages, as in German and Hebrew, the Moon is masculine while the Sun is feminine, which is directly opposite the view held today.

All trees were sacred to the Celts and Druids, including the oak, from which the word *druid* may have stemmed. An example of their close kinship with trees, in the Welsh "Cad Goddeau," the Britons magically shape-shifted into trees and defeated their enemies. The sacred trees of the Druids represented the spiritual ethos or nature of oneness. All trees symbolized the World Tree, with its connection to the Overworld, Middle World, and Underworld.

The oak, ash, and thorn, especially when growing close together, were considered potent magic. The Irish Druids more frequently referred to yew, hazel, and rowan trees. Some imply that the rowan, utilized in magical incantations, was the favored tree of the Druids. To facilitate prophetic visions, the Irish Druids slept on wattles of rowan. The action of climbing a tree or staying in one has often appeared in shamanistic traditions as a ritual gesture. In climbing a tree, the shaman embarks on an ecstatic journey.

No two trees are exactly the same and each tree has its own spirit personality that can be awakened and communicated with. Trees, because they live such long lives, are considered reservoirs of wisdom that can be tapped into when you know how. The Druids had this knowledge. Each sacred tree was associated with the Goddesses and Gods and thus with primeval archetypes.

The Druids had a kinship with these tree spirits and communed with them, gaining knowledge of the past and present. They knew which trees grew where and which trees were best used for fire, for making tools and weapons, for building houses, and so forth. The Druids used trees to mark sacred areas, such as their sacred groves. Attesting to the mixing and matching of esoteric traditions, Irish churches used to be called Dairthech, "oakhouse," which is the Druidic name for the sacred grove.

The ancient Druids were solitary dwellers in the forest, sometimes referred to as "boars." When they did gather together in groups, it was often in sacred groves, coming together to share philosophies and ideas, make laws, and discuss current issues. These groves were large circles of trees, often oak, apple, rowan, ash, or hazel trees, and frequently located on top of ley lines or natural energy centers.

More information is available on the Druidic connection with the oak than with other trees. For example, Pliny mentions that the Druids held nothing more sacred than the mistletoe and the tree that bears it, always supposing that tree to be the oak. He goes on to say that mistletoe, though commonly found on apple trees, only achieved sacred recognition when it graced the oak.

Red holly berries represented the drops of the life-giving lunar blood of the Goddess and were thus a fertility symbol, while the white mistletoe berries were drops of the oak God's semen and thus a phallic or sun symbol. The oak—in particular, mistletoe—acquired sexual significance, which still exists to this day as lovers kiss beneath it.

Pliny the Elder talks of the Druid ritual of cutting mistletoe on the sixth day of the Moon, followed by the sacrifice of two white bulls. He says the Druids cut the mistletoe with a golden sickle, catching it in a white cloth before it could touch the ground, but his account is colored by Roman idealizations. Also, mistletoe was not known in Ireland until the eighteenth century. Interestingly though, in modern Irish, it is known as *Druidh lus* or Druid's weed.

The oak was worshiped as a symbol of deity by all of the peoples who descended from the Indo-Europeans and was often referred to as the "Father of the Gods." The tree was an ancient phallic symbol and conveys divine omnipotence. The Goddess, in the form of water, nourished the oak and gave it birth.

With their roots in the food-gathering age—a time when thick, impenetrable oak forests covered Europe—Strabo says the Celts ate acorn bread as part of their regular diet. So not only did the oak provide food for the Celts but also fuel for warm fires and timber shelters from its flesh. In addition, oak was used in the mortuary constructions at both Le Tene and Hallstatt cultures of early Celtic society.

The Druids preferred groves of oaks for the sake of the tree alone and performed their rites in the presence of a branch of the oak. They felt that everything growing on the oak was sacred and divinely sent, proof that the tree was chosen by the God and Goddess themselves.

Throughout Europe and Asia Minor, the Druids worshiped in the open air under the trees. They avoided worshiping in buildings or temples. In fact, prior to the Roman Conquest, the Celts had never erected temples of worship. Instead, they felt that divine rapport was only accessible in the deep forests or in remote areas away from other people and the city-states of civilization. Features of geography and the very land itself held spiritual significance, and it was at these sacred and organic sites, often referred to as *nematons,* the Druids communed with nature. The Druids held religious rites and ceremonies in these *nematons.*

The classic composition of the *nemeton* is the residence of the sky God who controlled thunder and lightning, and who is also the deity of Druids and dryads (tree spirits). A Greek word, *nematon* describes a circular clearing in the midst of the woods that is a sort of mystical, terrestrial paradise or sylvan sanctuary. Thought of as a central opening of the world where divine and earthly worlds meet, usually the *nematon* is situated in a sacred forest grove consisting of oaks, sometimes mixed with other trees such as ash, rowan, birch, and so forth. Often a spring is next to the *nematon,* representing a link to the subterranean or Underworld. Druidic ceremonies took place in these clearings, physically and spiritually protected and sheltered by the trees. The natural grove of oaks drew the spirits of the Sky-World and the Otherworld, or Underworld, to the mortal or Middle World.

The modern Druid *nematon* is arranged with a pole or staff upright in the center, called "the bill." At its base to the south is the firepit (or holder) and to the north a cauldron of water, symbolizing the well. Usually a deep, narrow shaft is dug next to the well to receive offerings. These offerings represent the sacred meal of the Great Mother: silver for the well, oil for the fire, honey, red wine, apples, bread, salt, and ale.

The oak was *duir* (D) in the Druidic alphabet and represented power, as the oak is the hardiest and most useful of trees.

Robert Graves, in his book *The White Goddess,* postulates, "'The Song of Amergin' describes an ancient Celtic calendar alphabet and Druidic incantation, which summarizes a prime poetic myth relating to not only their ancestral origins, but to our own." No wonder the complex and magical Druidic order and Celtic traditions still fascinate us.

The Ogham

Popularly called the Druid Tree Alphabet, the Ogham (Ogam) was devised by the Irish Druids between the first and third centuries A.D., but some Celtic scholars think the Ogham to be of much greater antiquity, tracing similar inscriptions in Spain and Portugal from 500 B.C. The Celtic God of wisdom, literature, and eloquence, Ogma, is credited for inventing the Ogham alphabet. He was the son of the Good God, the Dagda, and a warrior and leader of the Tuatha De Danann. It was Ogma who captured the speaking sword of the Fomorian King Tethra.

The Ogham is a system of combining notches (vowels) and lines (consonants) together, which are drawn to, or cross, a baseline or midline called the "whale's back." Each letter consists of one to five slanted or vertical strokes, with vowels designated as notches or dots. The baseline is usually the edge of the object on which the Ogham inscription is carved or signed. The Shin, Hand, and Nose Ogham were kinds of a secret sign language used by the Druids, particularly useful at the negotiating table. The shin bone is the baseline in Shin Ogham, and the nose in the Nose Ogham. Both use the fingers to form the letters on the baseline. Pointing to, or showing certain finger joints to signify letters is used in Hand Ogham, or the letters are simply made by the fingers. Ogham messages were also spelled out by stringing the appropriate leaves in the correct order on a cord or a wooden wand, with "blank" leaves not included in the alphabet being used to divide one word from the next.

Oghams are read from top to bottom, and left to right, with each Ogham letter bearing the name of a tree or shrub, for example, B-Beth (Birch). The exceptions are the Sea (XI) and the Grove (CH). This reflects the Druids' strong affinity with the trees and nature. Not all of the Ogham plants were found in the Christian Celtic world of Britain. This strongly suggests that the Ogham predates the first century A.D. The region where the plants of the Ogham are best represented is the Rhine River Valley, home of the La Tene culture of the Iron Age. People of this culture are often referred to as being the ancestors of the Celts.

There are 369 Ogham inscriptions surviving today and this is only because they were carved in stone. They exist primarily in Ireland, but inscriptions are also scattered across Scotland, the Isle of Man, Wales, Cornwall, and England, and as far as Silchester, the tribal capital of the Celtic Atrebates. Similar carvings were also found in the state of West Virginia in the United States, which births the question whether the Celts came to the New World as early as 100 B.C.

That the Druidic teachings and practices were strictly oral and not written down is not entirely true. The Gaulish Druids only used Oghams for inscriptions, but according to Peter Ellis in his book *The Druids*, the Druidic prohibition on writing apparently did not extend to Ireland. In the Irish sagas and myths, there are several references to Druids reading and writing the Ogham. Druid libraries are frequently mentioned in the texts. For example, in the story, "The Voyage of Bran," Bran wrote down fifty or sixty quatrains of poetry in the Ogham. There were most likely large volumes of pagan books with ancient stories, poems, and sagas written down in the Ogham, which were later burned by the zealous, short-sighted Christian missionaries.

Akin to the runic alphabet, the Ogham was used for divination and as a sign language for communicating secret messages.

It was also used for recording stories, histories, and poetry, as well as genealogies, incantations, and spells. Ogham was a system of writing, with the alphabet divided into three subgroups: chieftains, peasants, and shrubs. Ogham is based upon a staff and using vertical and diagonal lines across this staff to form letters. For example, a Druid Bard carried a poet's staff, which was a staff made of several wooden wands, fastened at the bottom into a fan shape. It was on these wands that the Bards inscribed their tales. Oghams were also found in the Celtic libraries on the "rods of the Fili," which were wands made of hazel and aspen inscribed with the ancient stories.

Used for divination and foretelling the future, the Ogham or wisdom sticks were also magical Druidic tools. Modern day Pick-Up Sticks stem from Ogham sticks. If you decide to make your own Ogham sticks, verbally ask the tree permission before taking wood from it. Sticks are traditionally made of oak or another specially selected wood, blessed by saying a prayer, magical name, or chant over them, and then polished, notched with each Ogham, and then oiled with consecrated oil. One stick is left unnotched. To make your own Oghams, gather twenty-one same-sized sticks and carve or paint the Oghams on, one per stick. Place your Oghams in a bag or box. Ask for divine guidance and then think about your question. State your question out loud three times. Draw three, seven, or nine sticks without looking at them, or you can draw three sets of three if you like. Think about your question as you hold the sticks and then toss them onto the ground or table. The sticks closest to you represent current influences; sticks farthest from you symbolize the future outcome of your question. Any sticks that touch each other are related influences in regard to the question at hand.

The Oghams are still alive today and many of those who study the ancient traditions learn how to use them for writing and divination purposes. You can make your own or purchase Ogham sticks.

Ogham Chart

LETTER	NAME	TREE	THE OGHAM
B	Beith	Birch	
L	Luis	Rowan	
F	Fearn	Alder	
S	Saille	Willow	
N	Nuin	Ash	
H	Huathe	Hawthorn	
D	Duir	Oak	
T	Tinne	Holly	
C	Coll	Hazel	
Q	Quert	Apple	
M	Muin	Vine	
G	Gort	Ivy	
P or Ng	Pethboc/Ngetal	Dwarf Elder/Reed	
Ss	Straif	Blackthorn	
R	Ruis	Elder	
A	Ailim	Silver Fir	
O	Ohn	Furze	
U	Ur	Heather	
E	Eadha	White Poplar	
I	Idho	Yew	
Y	Too sacred to have a name	Mistletoe	

THE OGHAM VOWELS

A: Silver Fir (Ailim)
O: Furze (Onn)
U: Heather (Ur)
E: White Poplar (Eahha)
I: Yew (Idho)

THE OGHAM CONSONANTS

The consonants are related to the lunar calendar, the festival days, agricultural seasons, and tutelary deities. Robert Graves mentions that the letters of the modern Irish alphabet are similarly named after trees.

B: Birch (Beith)
L: Rowan (Luis)
N: Ash (Nion)
F: Alder (Fearn)
S: Willow (Saille)
H: Hawthorn (Uath)
D: Oak (Duir)
T: Holly (Tinne)
C: Hazel (Coll)
M: Vine (Muin)
G: Ivy (Gort)

P: Dwarf Elder (Pethboc)
R: Elder (Ruis)
Q: Apple (Quert)
Ng: Reed (NgEtal)
Ss: Blackthorn (Straif)
CH: Grove (Koad)
TH: Spindle (Oir)
PE: Honeysuckle (Uilleand)
PH: Beech (Phagos)
XI: The Sea (Mor)

The Ogham Trees

1. Birch—Beith

Seasonal Relationship: The Wolf Moon
Deities: Nemetona and Medb
Meaning: Rebirth, regeneration, pregermination, a new start and beginning. The birch has the "eyes" of the Goddess and was the Druid tree of the dead.

2. **Rowan—Luis**

   Seasonal Relationship: The Storm Moon, Bridget's Day
   Deities: Epona and Bridget
   Meaning: Rooting, germination, and fertilization by water; summoning; protection against enchantment. Rowan berries are the food of the Goddess and God.

3. **Alder—Fearn**

   Seasonal Relationship: The Chaste Moon, Hertha's Day
   Deities: Nimue, Arianrhod, and Bran the Blessed
   Meaning: Called the Faery Tree; oracular and protective; the bridge to the Otherworld; symbolizes purification by fire.

4. **Willow—Saille**

   Seasonal Relationship: The Seed Moon, Beltane
   Deities: Hertha, Coventina, Kerridwen, Morgana, and Tarvos
   Meaning: Giver of night vision; salicylic acid from its leaves and bark eases pain; represents flexibility, fertility, lunar rhythms, the coming of age, the poet tree.

5. **Ash—Nuin**

   Seasonal Relationship: The Hare Moon
   Deities: Etain, Gwydion, Math
   Meaning: Guardian Tree is associated with the runes, World Tree, the Otherworld, prophecy, water, rain, rivers, and the seas.

6. **Hawthorn—Huathe**

   Seasonal Relationship: The Dyad Moon
   Deities: Mei, Badb, and Cloidna
   Meaning: Protection of the harvest, purification, cleansing, and sacred union. Traditionally, the tree of the Faeries.

7. **Oak—Duir**

   Seasonal Relationship: The Mead Moon, Letha's Day
   Deities: Rhiannon, Artio, Bridget, Esus, Viviana, Myrddin, Dagda, Fergus, Robur
   Meaning: Strength, endurance, the ripening and harvest, success, protection, and trial by fire; the doorway to the mysteries and the boundary marker between worlds.

8. **Holly—Tinne**

   Seasonal Relationship: The Wort Moon, Lughnassad

   Deities: Viviana, Rosemerta, Lugh, and Bran

   Meaning: Knowledge, victory, promise and renewal of hope, rebirth, and divine wisdom; associated with the Green Knight.

9. **Hazel—Coll**

   Seasonal Relationship: The Barley Moon

   Deities: Fliodhas and Sadv

   Meaning: Clear sight, mystic wisdom, healing, magical ability and magical wands, measurement, purifying, intuition, self-honesty, poetry, and meditative states; the tree of the Sidhe and of divination used by dowsers.

10. **Apple—Quert**

    Seasonal Relationship: The Barley Moon

    Deities: Danu, Amaethon, and Rhiannon

    Meaning: The fertile Celtic Tree of Life; the Tree of Avalon that is the window to the Otherworld; associated with knowledge, eternal life, and the choice between inner and outer beauty. In Celtic myth, red, green, and golden apples represent stages of spiritual development.

11. **Vine—Muin**

    Seasonal Relationship: The Wine Moon, Hellith's Day

    Deities: Damona, Nantosuelta, Lugh, and Myrddin

    Meaning: Harvest, plenty, peace, prophecy, clarity of awareness; associated with the way through: roads, paths, keys, the spiral, gates, and doors.

12. **Ivy—Gort**

    Seasonal Relationship: The Blood Moon

    Deities: Andraste, Morgana, and Bran

    Meaning: Sacred plant of darkness, passage to Otherworlds, clarity, strength, self-sacrifice, and the active search and discovery of one's self through introspection.

13. **Reed—Ngetal**

    Seasonal Relationship: The Snow Moon, Samhain

Deities: Sirona, the Dagda, and Borvos

Meaning: Healing ability, spiritual awareness, perception, flexibility, and durability; associated with the healing power of music.

14. **Blackthorn—Straif**

Seasonal Relationship: Samhain

Deities: The Morrigan, Badb, and Macha

Meaning: Cleansing, healing, death, and piercing self-reflection. The more one struggles, the deeper the thorns cut.

15. **Elder—Ruis**

Seasonal Relationship: The Oak Moon, Yule

Deities: Danu, Gabba, and Kerridwen

Meaning: Emblem of the Great Pattern, the Druid College, and the *Nematon,* representing the endless Celtic weave— forever-ending, forever-beginning.

16. **Silver Fir (or the Elm)—Ailim**

Seasonal Relationship: The first day of the new year, after Yule

Deities: The Maid, Mother, and Crone

Meaning: The Mother Tree associated with insight, spiritual progress, the silvering wheel or woman and feminine rebirth, sexuality, childbirth, and the threefold aspect of the Goddess.

17. **Furze (also the Gorse or Broom)—Ohn**

Seasonal Relationship: Hertha's Day, culminating with Beltane

Deities: Viviana, Mei, Artio, and Tarvos

Meaning: Gathering resources for the journey ahead; the greening, the mating season, fertility, and growth.

18. **Heather (or Lime or Linden)—Ur**

Seasonal Relationship: Letha's Day

Deities: Blodenwedd, Sirona, Rosemerta, Hellith

Meaning: Sexual ecstasy, the divine love of the Goddess and God, mastery of the elements; associated with the Queen Bee and the Otherworld.

19. **White Poplar (or Aspen)—Eadha**

Seasonal Relationship: Lughnassad and Hellith's Day

Deities: Lugh, Gobannon, Creidne, and Taillte

Meaning: The ancient Shieldmaker's Tree, prevents illness, helps in rebirth, and eases stress; linked to the Celtic Oral tradition.

20. Yew (or Juniper)—Idho

Seasonal Relationship: The Death of the Year

Deities: The Morrigan, Badb, Danu, Banba, Sucellos, and Gwyn ap Nudd

Meaning: Adaptability, flexibility, strength, and access of memories. An Ancestral Tree associated with the crescent moon, the bow, and rebirth, the Yew represents overcoming one's conditioning.

21. The Grove—Koad

Seasonal Relationship: The first day of the Dyn Du Gwrach or Days of Sorrow

Deities: Nematona, Gabba, Medb, and Belenus

Meaning: Drynemeton, associated with the number thirteen, knowledge, sacred springs, woods, and sacred places.

22. Spindle—Oir

Seasonal Relationship: The second day of the Dyn Du Gwrach, or the Days of Sorrow

Deities: Gabba and Taranis

Meaning: Sudden intelligence and insight, a flash of enlightenment, and completion of the task at hand; associated with the wheel of the seasons and self-responsibility.

23. Honeysuckle—Uilleand

Seasonal Relationship: The third day of the Dyn Du Gwrach, or Days of Sorrow

Deities: Gabba, Danu, Rosemerta, Angus Og

Meaning: Associated with flight, the source of the wren and the lapwing, the honeysuckle reveals hidden secrets and future patterns; used for protection and gaining insight.

24. Beech—Phagos

Seasonal Relationship: The fourth day of the Dyn Du Gwrach, or Days of Sorrow

Deities: Gabba, Cordemannon, Ogma, and Gwydion

Meaning: As Father of the Oak, the beech represents the Great Book of the Art and Craft; rules ancient heirlooms, inheritance, and talents like second sight.

25. The Sea—Mor

Seasonal Relationship: The fifth or last day of the Dyn Du Gwrach, or Days of Sorrow; called the "Nameless Day" (*di-enwidydd,* or "without naming day"), associated with the winter solstice or the day when the Sun is at its lowest point or appears "dead."

Deities: Gabba, Llyr, and Manannan

Meaning: Travel, maternal lineage, associated with the crane, the new sun, the setting sun, and the primordial sea.

The Druid Grove Creative Visualization

The purpose of this creative visualization is to attune yourself with the sacred land and the three worlds, the Upper World, Middle World, and Underworld. Read through the following visualization two or three times, following along as if it is you moving through the sequence of events. Next, I strongly suggest you tape record the visualization, using your own voice and playing it back while sitting or lying in a comfortable place, somewhere you will not be disturbed by others or the telephone. The optimum time to listen to your tape recording is just before you go to sleep and just upon waking.

Begin by breathing deeply and rhythmically. Breathe in to the count of three, holding your breath for three counts, and then exhale to the count of three. Visualize and sense brilliant white light filling your body as you breathe in, and let any negativity or tension leave your body, mind, and spirit as you exhale. Breathe this way for a few minutes, making yourself as comfortable as possible, loosening any clothing, stretching out, flexing any tense muscles, and then relaxing your body completely, becoming more and more calm and peaceful with each exhaling breath.

Listen to the rhythm of your breath and sense your heart beating like a drum at the core of your being. Allow your eyes to close slowly and completely, relaxing even more as you continue to breathe to the count of three. In your mind's eye, begin the journey by seeing and sensing yourself standing in a thick forest on May Day. There are tall and mighty oaks and sinuous ash trees, with small wild daisies covering the forest floor. You can hear the birds in the tree canopy and the sound of a stream running nearby. You can sense the power in the land all around you, energizing you. The fresh scent of the trees, earth, and water washes over you, carried in the soft morning breeze. A thin white fog fills the forest, the mist shining silver as the sun's morning rays slice through it. The glistening mist brushes against you like a cat and slowly surrounds and enfolds you, oddly relaxing you as it gently swirls over your feet, legs, torso, limbs, and up over your head. The silver mist rolls in above and below you, before, beside, and behind you. You can feel the moisture cooling your face and taste the tiny droplets of morning dew within the shining mist on your lips.

The fog grows thicker and more cloud-like, and you feel as if you are floating in the forest, being lifted on a silvery-white cloud and sailing through the woods like a boat cutting through the water. You can feel yourself being pulled as if by a current, being carried faster and faster. Spirit beings of light flash by you and ancestral faces appear and then disappear just as quickly. You see faces of people you have known and you sense their presence for a moment or two as you sail on through the woods.

An opening in the thick forest appears before you. Light streams across the top of the forest opening, and a blackish cloud flows across its bottom. You sail in between the light and darkness, through a window of destiny and into another dimension of time and space. You are neither here nor there, but afloat in some Otherworld of timelessness. You sense yourself simultaneously swimming in the sea like a dolphin, flying through the sky like a hawk, running across the land like a wolf, and feeding in a lush green meadow like a deer.

The silver mist around you begins to dissolve, and you slowly drift to a halt, gently touching down on solid ground in a forest clearing. The last of the mist twinkles in the sun's rays and then disappears altogether in the soft breeze, unveiling the hidden land you have entered.

You look around to see a distinct path, lined with large milky white quartz boulders, that leads to the edge of the clearing. You follow the path slowly, looking up at the sky briefly as you go, and noticing that the light seems more silvery than golden. Most of all you notice an absence of sound. Even the breeze as it moves through the trees seems silent.

The path leads you to a crossroads consisting of a central hub of white quartz stones. From this hub are three similar paths. You follow the middle path to a magnificent grove of oak trees, encircled by hundreds of large milky stones. A stag and doe eat the long tufts of green grass that grow around the base of the largest oak in the grove. The intricate weaving of its roots echo the pattern of the universe. The pattern interlocks and repeats over and over between the tree and the Earth. As you look upward, you spy a marvelous eagle perched near the top of the oak on a leafless branch.

You can see, smell, and hear the small stream flowing close to the grove, feeding the oaks with the primal waters of life. The water weaves through the grove, flowing along the veins of the Mother Goddess, and over the gnarled roots of the giant oaks. You can see squirrels running in and out of the trees' out-stretched branches.

The massive oak near the grazing deer is larger than any other tree in the grove. It stands at a crossroads in the hidden forest grove, and its roots and branches reach out everywhere in all directions, below and above.

You move over to the base of the oak, and the deer continue

feeding. Looking up at the immense green canopy, you begin to walk clockwise around the massive tree trunk. You circle around the oak three times and then stop in front of it. Kneeling down, you touch the ground at the oak's base with the palms of your hands, feeling the coolness of the Earth. Taking a deep breath, you slowly glide your hands upward and softly touch the bark of the massive tree in front of you. For a moment you become the tree and you cannot tell where your hands stop and the bark of the tree starts. You feel yourself rising from out of the Mother Earth. The energy of the Earth moves into your feet, legs, spine, belly, heart, torso, limbs, and head. Breathing the power and energy from the Earth into your body energizes and centers you. Merging with the tree, you feel your feet deeply rooted in the ground. You sense a long tap root shooting down from your feet through the stones and Earth, finally touching the cool, deep waters beneath the ground. With each breath, you sense the water coursing up through your roots and flowing through your feet and up through your body, refreshing and revitalizing you. Your trunk feels thick and strong, and your limbs branch out, creating an all-reaching gate to the sky.

At one with the oak, you stand like the great World Tree at the spiritual center of the universe. You still feel your hands resting on the rough tree bark, and gently you take your right hand and tap the tree trunk nine times: one-two-three, one-two-three, one-two-three. As you do this, the tree trunk opens up and reveals a hidden passage. The hush of the forest around you becomes more pronounced. You feel a blast of hot air, and then suddenly from out of the belly of the oak comes a power-ful man with stormy grey eyes and skin the color of bark. His silver-white hair, moustache, and beard are tangled with mistle-toe. He wears a long bark-colored robe with a leaf-green cloak over his shoulders. His feet are bare. As he speaks, the sound of his voice resonates deep within, taking you one minute past eternity and back again in a single moment. He says, "I am

Robur, the God of Oaks. I am the divine revealer. I shape beauty to human mouths, and I give wings to insight. I guard the threshold of worlds, and wait for those who come."

He removes his leaf-green cloak and places it over your shoulders. As you pull the cloak around your body, you are also pulled into the belly of the oak and into the womb of the tree itself. You pass through a long, dark tunnel where all of your memories and deepest hopes and desires flood through your mind and flow just as quickly back out again. As if you are journeying to the center of the Earth, you are pulled farther down, and then farther still, through the dark tunnel.

You find yourself in a dim underground chamber that opens up into a large, brighter chamber. At the center of the large chamber is a small pool of water, fed by a natural spring. The roots of the oak seem to weave over and into the water. Next to the pool is a natural granite altar, set with a lit candle and incense, as well as a bowl of herbs and oils, a clear quartz crystal, and a cup filled with liquid.

A woman cloaked in brown stands next to the altar, looking into the pool of water. She kneels down and puts her head between her knees with her forehead touching the ground, her cloak pulled completely over her. You move closer to the woman and quietly watch her for a few moments. She stands back up, turns around, and looks directly at you before speaking, "I am Coventina, the Goddess of the sacred well, the well of all possibilities. The well is the storehouse of all knowledge and wisdom, the deep gate that flows within and without."

She bends down and picks up a handful of soil. Tossing it into the pool, she beckons you to do the same. Coventina smiles, her brown eyes sparkling as she tells you, "Remember, half of the learning is already in your head and all the knowing is already in your soul." Then she hands you the cup of liquid. You pour the clear liquid over the roots of the oak that weave into the clear pool. As the liquid meets the roots of the oak, you suddenly find yourself transported upward and out of the belly of the oak and into the topmost branches of the mighty tree.

You reach out as if to touch the sky and the brilliant Sun shining overhead. The Sun's warmth fills you as you raise your arms to the sky. Continuing to reach upward, you also gaze upward. Your vision shifts and the Sun becomes like a fire Goddess, bright eyed with honey-colored hair and golden robes. She winds a golden thread upon a silver spindle. From the fingers of her hand come five streams of fiery light. The streams of light surge toward you, touching your head, arms, and legs, and everywhere the light touches you feels bright and warm. The fire Goddess speaks, "I am Bridget, keeper of the sacred flame, the shape-fire. I inspire and spark all those who arrive at this crossroads between worlds."

She transforms into a hundred and one brilliant beams of light, and each one of her warm rays penetrate your branches, body, and roots, filling your entire being with inspiration and light, healing warmth, and divine radiance. You can feel the sacred fire, the living, creative spirit of the sun burning within you.

You look around the forest grove from your vantage point high in the branches of the massive oak. You soak in the vision of the hidden Otherworldly forest, focusing on the many details and your connection to those you have met on your journey. Give thanks to the powers of the sky above the Earth, to the sacred land, and to the spirits within it. Carry the strength and connection with the powers of the Tree, Well, and Fire as they grow, flow, and flame within you every moment of every day. As you breathe deeply, integrating your experiences, the mist gathers and begins to engulf you. You find yourself wrapped in the mist and floating through the thick dense silver-white fog.

Breathe deeply, feeling centered and connected with the Earth, Water, and Sun. The mist thins and disappears and you begin to come back to the room, moving your legs, feet, and toes, arms, hands, and fingers around, and finally completely returning to your body and the present moment. Open your eyes and take a few minutes to stretch your arms and legs, all the while thinking about your visualization experience. Write down your impressions of being the oak and of the three worlds of Sky, Earth, and Well—Overworld, Middle World, and Underworld.

4

THE FAERIES

I caught him at work one day, myself,
In the castle-ditch, where foxglove grows,—
A wrinkled, wizen'd and bearded Elf,
Spectacles stuck on his pointed nose,
Silver buckles to his hose,
Leather apron—shoe in his lap—
"Rip-rap, tip-tap,
Tick-tack-too!
(A grasshopper on my cap!
Away the moth flew!)"

From "The Leprachaun; or Fairy Shoemaker"
by William Allingham

Origins of the Faery

In every culture, there are stories of beings that have super-natural or magical abilities and share human characteristics, beings that can greatly influence the daily lives of mortals. Dwelling on earth in close contact with mortals, generally such faeries are invisible, sometimes helpful and benevolent, occasionally dangerous and frightening, and other times playful and mischievous. In fact, most of the stories about the Faery are actually traditions that relate real beliefs of the people, and hidden within the tales are many of the key elements of ancient mystery traditions.

The etymology (root) of the word *Faery* (Faerie) is Middle French, from the Old French word *fee*, also spelled *feie*, which stems from the Late Latin *fata* (the Goddess of fate), and from the Latin *fatum*, meaning "fate." In Middle English, *faery* or *fay* had three meanings: one, enchantment; two, a land where enchanted beings lived; or three, the group of inhabitants of such a place. The current definition of Faery is a mythical being of folklore and romance with human form and magical powers.

The Irish word for faery is *sidheog* (little Faery), from the word *side* or *shee*, as in "banshee." The word *sidh* is the Celtic root for a blast of wind. They are called the *daoine sidhe*, or the Faery people, or the *aos side*, the people of the mounds. The Faeries ride their milk-white Faery horses and are accompanied by their Faery hounds. The Faery folk are the gentry, famous for the music that lures mortals out of this world (*ceol side*), the Faery mist (*ceo side*), whirling winds (*seidean side*), a Faery sleep from which you cannot wake until the appointed time, and Faery stroke or elf-shot (*poc side*).

Beings most often called the Faeries (fairies, fays, or fae) are found across the world, more frequently in Europe and Asia and less often in Africa and America. I prefer using the term *Faery* because it is the traditional name used by those in the Faery tradition. Faery means "the bright people" or simply "the people."

Faeries are more common in Irish than in English traditions, although they are also popular in Scotland, Wales, Lancashire, and Cornwall. There are over seventy Irish townships beginning with "shee," and the Irish people often refer to the *shee* as the gentry, because of their tall, noble appearance and silvery sweet speech. Ireland abounds with places having Faery associations such as the Sheegys, the Faery hill in Donegal, the Faery woods in Sligo, and the Sheeauns, the Faery mounds. James Joyce once said that parts of Connaught were more thickly populated with Faeries than with mortals.

By region, the Faeries are called the Feens or Fians of the Scottish Highlands and Ireland, the Pechs of the Lowlands, the Trows of Shetland, and the Manx call the Faery *sleigh beggey* (little folk), the li'l fallas, or Ferrishyn. Female Faeries were also called the *y mammau* (the mothers), linking them to the pagan Celtic deities, the "Matres." Other names of the Faeries are "Side," "Sidhe," "Sidei," "Sighe," "Sith," "Sidhe Sith Si," "Sheoques," "Tylwyth teg" (the fair family), "Duine Matha," and the Good People.

Among the Celts, there survives the belief of an invisible realm inhabited by Otherworldly beings known collectively as the *Sidhe* or the Good People. This belief was once common throughout all the Celtic countries in localized forms. The Sidhe exist simultaneously with mortal humans along the cosmic continuum. Even though the Sidhe (Faery) are thought to be a distinct race, quite separate from human beings, they have had much contact with mortals over the centuries.

Some scholars argue that even though the Faeries are linked to the Druids and the Bards, they are considerably older than the Druids, reaching back to the remotest antiquity. Some say they are the surviving members of an ancient race of beings that inhabited the British Isles during the Neolithic period (6000–1800 B.C.). The Faery came into the forefront when mortals changed from nomadic hunters into agrarian farmers and herders, staying in one place for several generations. The strength of the Faery stems from the land, a land made sacred through the generations of ancestors buried in it.

Belief in the Faery race, who possess powers beyond those of mortals, who can move quickly through the air and change their shape at will, once played a huge part in the lives of people living in rural Ireland and Scotland. Considered to be the spirits of the old agricultural Goddesses and Gods of the Earth, the Sidhe of the subterranean mounds controlled the ripening of the crops and the milk yields. Therefore, offerings of milk and other foods were routinely given to Sidhe.

The Celts respected the Sidhe and felt that building on the invisible Faery paths, called *trods,* that ran from one mound (Faery rath, fort, or royalty) to another would bring bad luck. The Faery raths are small fields enclosed by circular ditches, thought to be sheepfolds and dwellings of the Faeries. A *trod* is a line of a different shade of green in the fields. The *trod* goes in a straight line similar to a ley line, which indicates an energetic flow within the land itself. The Irish saying "in the way" means that something is obstructing a *trod,* a passageway, or is violating some place preempted by the Sidhe. In fact, when a house is built "in the way" it frequently burns down or the people in it die. If a barn is erected on such a spot, often the animals in it die. Again, this points to morphogenic fields and the probability that Faery paths may be grids of negative ley lines, which are polarities of energies that adversely affect animals, including humans.

The origins of Faery lore are difficult to pinpoint. Many writers maintain that the people of Ireland and their Gods before the coming of the Gaels are the "ancestors" of the Sidhe. The first use of the term *sidhe* was as a means of identifying the Bronze Age Tuatha De Danann after their defeat by the Milesians (the first Gaels).

The Sons of Mil (Milesians) arrived in Ireland and found the Tuatha De Danann (the people of the Goddess Dana) in control of the land. The Sons of Mil fought the Tuatha, defeating and driving them underground, where it is said they remain to this day in the hollow hills or Sidhe mounds. These first occupants of the Faery underworld became the "Daoine Sidhe," the very cream of the heroic Faeries.

As the Tuatha De Danann divided the hills and mounds of Ireland into kingdoms among themselves, they simultaneously wove a permanent veil of invisibility for themselves, thus dividing Ireland into two kingdoms, the seen and the unseen. In terms of modern physics, they created a new morphogenic field of resonance or vibration just beyond the spectrum of normal human perception.

Faeries are the sacred spirit or presence that animates and enlivens all of nature. Regarded as earth spirits, the "Sidhe-dwellers" are the land Faeries and are called the *dei terreni,* meaning deities of the Earth. The water Faeries, called Merrows, are thought to bring bad weather; they come out of the sea in the shape of hornless cows or humans with fish tails.

Often the Faeries are also considered the ancient ancestors, made up of distinct tribes. Each tribe's Faeries have personal names (not necessarily Tuatha names) and rule over specific areas. Each area or territory has a Faery queen and king; for instance, Finnbeara is the king of the Faeries of Connacht. In this way, the social order to the Sidhe reflects the old aristocracy of ancient Ireland.

Unquestionably, the belief in the Faery is part of a pagan, pre-Christian religion. Within the Faery lore of Scotland and Ireland are the remnants of the old pagan religion, with Gods and Goddesses being remembered as the guardian ancestors of the clans. All the clans once claimed descent from a particular deity. These same pagan Goddesses and Gods appear in local tales, transformed into Faery kings and queens. For example, Medb is a heroine of Irish epic and later becomes Queen Medb of the Faeries. Living in Faery palaces as guardians of lakes, rivers, and certain locales, the pagan deities now transformed as Faeries are still a part of the land and the folk memory of the people.

Another example of the pagan deities transforming into Faeries is the Lady of the Lake, the mysterious woman who gave King Arthur his sword, Excalibur. She is identical to Morgan Le Fay, who is closely associated with, if not an off-shoot of, the Celtic Goddess Morgana. The Celtic Goddess of fertility and death, Morgana is directly associated with the Mor-rigan, and both are Goddesses of great antiquity, representing the sovereignty of the land.

Several strands of thought intertwine, but most agree that the Faery are beings halfway between the material and spiri-tual, mortal and deity, who are occasionally seen but interact freely with mortals. They are thought to be a real race of invis-ible or spiritual beings living in their own dimensional realm, usually invisible to us. Because the Faeries are always near us and listen without being seen, it is always wise to speak well of them.

In his book *The Living World of Faery*, R. J. Stewart writes, "Faeries are living beings which are one step, one change of awareness, beyond humanity." In this sense, the Faery are one step away from our reality, normally just out of our range of perception. Perhaps this is the reason many times I only catch a glimpse of the Faeries out of the corner of my eye. When I do see the Faery images clearly, it seems as soon as I move, blink, or even change my thoughts, the Faery vanishes. Often my cat will look with rapt attention at the same spot. I have noticed that there are certain times of the day that are better for catch-ing a glimpse of the Faeries. These four times are: (1) in the hour just before sunrise, (2) noon, (3) twilight, and (4) midnight. In my experience, just before sunrise and at twilight are the best times for communicating with and seeing the Faeries.

I have also found that the Faeries are conscious beings of energy that seem to dwell in another realm or dimensional sphere in the universe. Sometimes, the door or threshold to the Faery realm is open and at that time contact occurs. The Faeries visit but only briefly. I personally do not use terms such as "Little People" or "Small Folk" because the Faeries that I encounter are not small by any means, but are human size and often much larger. They are my co-walkers, allies, guardians, and guides.

Many people from all walks of life, young and old, have had experiences with the Faeries. Those with second sight are apt to see the Faeries any time. The Faery are the closest beings to us on the spiritual level and are attuned to the land and considered the spirits of a place, or *genii locii*. In Celtic culture, deities often took localized form, although the more powerful and independent Faeries were mobile and could travel great distances. Although their power remained the same, their names, attributes, and other expressions were modified through time.

Robert Kirk, a Scottish Episcopalian minister, scholar, and seventh son, wrote the *Secret Commonwealth of Elves, Fauns and Fairies* in the late seventeenth century, still a primary source for Highland Faery lore and second sight. He is thought to be entrapped in the Faery realm, a victim of "Faery (elf) stroke." He had a habit of wandering around the Faery hills at night and one morning he was found on the Fairy Knowe of the Sith Bruach at Aberfoyle. He was unconscious and had to be carried to bed. Kirk died without regaining consciousness but is said to still be active in the Faery realm.

Author R. J. Stewart is probably the leading living authority on the Faery tradition. He has written many books and articles, sharing his experiences with the Faeries and providing hands-on techniques for communicating with the Faeries and journeying into the Underworld of the Faery. R. J. Stewart's work demonstrates that even though the Faery tradition is of greatest antiquity, the elements and teachings are still relevant and useful today.

In pre-Christian times, people believed Faeries were the spirits of the dead or deified mortals. The Manx belief is that it was unlucky to use the word *Faery,* and they instead used the terms *themselves, they,* or *them that's in it,* to refer to Faeries, believing that "themselves" are the souls of those drowned in Noah's Flood.

In post-Christian times, Faeries were typecast as fallen angels and occasionally as astral or elemental spirits. With the growth of Puritanism in seventeenth-century England, the view of Faeries became darker and the fallen angels began to be regarded as evil.

Some theories suggest that Faery beliefs were founded on the memory of a primitive race of people driven into hiding by invaders. In this sense, the Faery are the folk memories of the original inhabitants of the land, lingering in the mountains, rivers, and hills.

When thought of as spirits of the dead, Faeries fall under certain types, examples being the Sluagh, or Faery Hosts, who according to Highland belief are the evil dead who rode on the wind. In another example, Finnbeara's Faeries were both the recent and ancient dead. In Cornwall, the Small People are the heathen dead and the Piskies are the souls of babies, appearing at twilight in the form of white moths. According to Kirk, the Faery knowes by the churchyard were supposed to be places where the souls of the dead lodged, awaiting the Day of Judgment.

The Sluagh, or the Host of the Unforgiven Dead, are the most formidable of the Highland Faery people. Some regard "The Host" not as the dead but as fallen angels. Others regard the Host as the spirits of mortals who have died. Still others distinguish between the Faeries and the Host. Generally, the Faeries are to be seen after or about sunset and move about on the ground, whereas the Host travel at midnight in the air, riding the wind, above places inhabited by mortals.

Robert Kirk called the Highland Faeries "Subterraneans," and the Highlanders believe the Faeries are spirits of their ancestors. The Faery hills, or *brochs,* that these beings live in are the homes of the Highlanders' dead ancestors and are therefore sacred.

The term *White Ladies*, designating both ghosts and Faeries, is yet another connection between *Faeries* and the dead. The supernatural elements in early Arthurian legends show that *Guinevere* originally meant "white phantom," having the same meaning as the Irish *Bean Fhionn*, or White Lady of Lough Gur, who claims a human life every seven years. The White Ladies draw close at the time of death and bear the soul to its Faery home. The White Ladies are the direct descendants of the fabled Tuatha De Danann, the ancient Goddesses and Gods.

Most who follow the Faery tradition agree that Faeries are the immortal polytheistic group of Goddesses and Gods of pagan Ireland who have merged with the land, such as the Daoine Sidhe and Tylwyth Teg. Irish mythology tells the tale of the Good God Dagda, who assigned the Tuatha De Danann each one of the Faery mounds, or Sidhe. These are the Otherworldly kingdoms, beneath the fields and hills of the land, and within and beneath the rivers, lakes, and streams. The Faery people continue to thrive underground, in the caves and hollow hills of the countryside. Their knowledge and wisdom of nature, and their supernatural powers, can be called upon and used by humankind.

Similarities are found in the Faery lore of Scotland, due to the migration of peoples back and forth between Scotland and Ireland. The last wave of Gaelic incomers into Scotland from Ireland was in the fifth century, but for many centuries before this the Irish were intermarrying with the Cruithne (Picts) of Scotland. There has been a long history of exchange between the two lands, leading to a blending of folklore and beliefs.

In the west of Ireland, where the native Irish were driven ("to hell or Connaught"), the people have held onto their ancient heritage much longer than most peoples in the world. Even though Christianity became the predominant religion in Ireland, the Faery faith continues to thrive, especially now, with the renewed interest in paganism and the Faery tradition. The

Faeries are still seen, with Faery anecdotes turning up throughout Great Britain and the world.

The Otherworld Kingdoms of the Faery

The Faery have Otherworldly palaces and kingdoms where they feast and play music, and are known to battle with neighboring tribes. They arise from the hills and mounds on the eves of Beltane, Midsummer, and Samhain to walk among mortals. The Faery live in houses furnished lavishly with gold and silver. They eat great banquets and feasts of exotic and delicious food. The common belief is that any mortal who eats or drinks anything in the Faery realm can never return to his or her home. There are stories of children who are lured to the Faery mounds and are stopped just in time from eating the food offered them. Others say that if you eat some Faery food, you will be gifted with second sight and forever have the power to see the Faeries.

Birth exists in the Faery realm, but not death. There are stories of Faery children, of Faeries searching for mortal women to nurse them, and of abductions of mortal midwives to attend Faery births.

Stories of these mysterious Otherworlds or magical realms abound in Celtic mythology and folklore, with many heroic tales and adventures happening in these elemental kingdoms. These lands are the home of our emotive primordial links with our origins, the home of all knowledge and universal wisdom.

The Faery realm mirrors the mortal realm. Whatever is found in one world has a reflection or polar partner in the other. The Celtic people believed that beyond the "ordinary world," there were veils upon veils of conscious beings such as the Faeries, who have no inherent form but shape-shift at will.

The Celts were ancestor worshipers, and their deities were also the ancestors of the clan. Many stories and legends center around the explanation of how these ancestors made perilous journeys into the Otherworld realms in order to perform a task or undergo some sort of transformation.

The Faeries live on the astral plane and in Otherworlds of varying levels of reality. The Otherworld is everywhere, within and around us. To fully understand the concept of the Otherworld, you have to let go of your linear perceptions and view reality as layered: dimension upon dimension, realm upon realm. The Otherworlds of experience are realms that exist energetically or experientially—as R. J. Stewart says, "a step beyond your awareness."

Time and space, time and space and energy, and time and space and form are all relative. Appearance, reality, and identity are also relative and very different according to one's point of view. In this way, your identity, location, and reality are relative and are shifting and changing all of the time, just as everything shifts and changes every moment. The location of the Otherworld is also relative and can be accessed, depending upon the relative location of your consciousness. The Otherworld is ever-present. It's just that your attention is here, not there in the Otherworld. The exciting thing is you can learn to be both here and there at the same time, relatively present, experientially speaking, in both realms.

When you perceive life on three planes—physical, mental, and spiritual—woven together as one (as reflected in Celtic triadic symbols such as the triple-headed image and the triskele), the idea of Otherworlds becomes easier to understand. As you realize that spirit exists on all levels of awareness, Otherworlds seem like different threads of the same fabric.

To move into the Faery realm or dimension does not necessarily require you to enter through any geographical point. A Fairy ring, the encounter with the Fairy Host, the singing of the wind, or even stepping upon turf with a Faery spell called the *stray sod,* can sometimes trigger the experience of finding yourself in the Faery realm, where time and space alter.

Where there is an entryway or portal leading into the Underworld of the Faery realm, it almost always includes a Faery ring or circle. The folk belief is that such rings are dancing places of the Faery. A Faery ring is usually made of a circle of mushrooms produced at the periphery of a body of mycelium, growing outward, or it consists of a ring of dark green vegetation, especially when associated with mushrooms. Other portals to the Faery realm are an opening at the roots of a large tree, a hollow in an old tree, a cave, an opening in the ground, and an underground cistern. It is unwise to interfere with the portals to the Faery realm, and only enter them if you know what you are doing. In one Irish folktale, a mortal man was taken to the Faery realm and 900 years passed as if it were one night.

Seasons also figure into mortal and Faery contact, as the doors to the Faery palaces are wide open on Beltane, Midsummer, and Samhain. Also, certain days of the week figure into the process, as do the four hinges of the day: early dawn, noon, dusk, and midnight. During certain times of the year, generally on the Eight Great Days and Full Moons, the portals between the Faery and mortal dimensions of existence are easier to see and move through for both mortals and the Faeries.

The Eight Great Days—Path of the Sun

1. Yule, winter solstice at 00.00 degrees Capricorn
2. Bridget's Fire, Feb. 2nd (or at 15.00 degrees Aquarius)
3. Hertha's Day, spring equinox at 00.00 degrees Aries
4. Beltane, May 1st (or at 15.00 degrees Taurus)
5. Letha's Day, summer solstice at 00.00 degrees Cancer
6. Lughnassad, 1st week of August (or at 15.00 degrees Leo)
7. Hellith's Day, autumnal equinox at 00.00 degrees Libra
8. Samhain, October 31st (or at 15.00 degrees Scorpio)

THE THIRTEEN FULL MOONS—PATH OF THE MOON
(Begin with the first Full Moon after Yule.)

1. Wolf Moon
2. Storm Moon
3. Chaste Moon
4. Seed Moon
5. Hare Moon
6. Dyad Moon
7. Mead Moon
8. Wort Moon
9. Barley Moon
10. Wine Moon
11. Blood Moon
12. Snow Moon
13. Oak Moon

Note: The Oak Moon is not used in twelve full moon years.

More important than whether they are physical or not, these portals or thresholds are experiential and exist at the key centers of your being. Carefully walking through them can lead to lasting personal transformation and change. The moments you are most relaxed and at one with everything are often the times when you journey to the many realms and Otherworlds of the Faery. In the Faery realm there is no death, no age, no sickness, and no ugliness.

The mists will clear as you enter elemental kingdoms such as Tirfo Thuinn, the Land Under the Waves still seen today. Jan Morris writes in her book *A Matter of Wales* of just such a land:

It appears to mortals, now and then, who stand upon a particular patch of ground in the village of Llanon in Wales, on the gently sloping hillside a mile or two above the sea: and if you wait outside the post office on a suitable morning, on one of those grey-green patchy, illusory Welsh mornings when nothing is quite distinct, even your own perceptions— if you wait there on such a day in the right frame of mind, presently you may just make out, not far offshore, the dim green form of some other country, half awash in the tide, and rippled with white waves. Some people claim to hear bells and music, when the wind is right: others can see and hear nothing at all.

Another well-known Otherworld is the Land of the Young, Tir-nan-Og. Also called the land of beauty and home to the Tuatha De Danann, Tir-nan-Og lies west across the sea. It is an Earthly paradise where death never enters and time is no longer reckoned by mortal measures; where the grass is always green and fruit and flowers are continuously blooming; where feasting and merry making go on all day and night.

The Isle of the Blest, called Hy-Brasail, is another Celtic Otherworld. Gerald Griffin's poem called "Hy-Brasail—The Isle of the Blest"—describes this magical realm:

> On the ocean that hollows the rocks where ye dwell,
> A shadowy land has appeared, as they tell;
> Men thought it a region of sunshine and rest,
> And they called it Hy-Brasail, the isle of the blest.
> From year unto year on the ocean's blue rim,
> The beautiful spectre showed lovely and dim;
> The golden clouds curtained the deep where it lay,
> And it looked like an Eden, away, far away!

Types of Faeries

"There are many classes or orders of the People of Light, with their own habits, lives, structure of tribe, family, and the like. Some are well known to mortal men and women, others are invisible and hidden away, yet they will emerge at certain times if bidden appropriately," writes R. J. Stewart in *The Living World of the Faery*.

The Fairies are the elemental powers of the land, the ancient Earth-Shapers who live in the hollow hills, and to whom the mortal world is but a dream. They are the spirits associated with rivers, lakes, hills, trees, streams, caves, and sacred sites. The Faeries of the Earth and the Sea are gentle and beautiful creatures who will do no harm when left alone and are allowed to dance on the Faery raths in the moonlight to sweet music, undisturbed by the presence of mortals.

The same type of Faeries will appear differently from culture to culture, due to the fact that they take their physical forms from the human imagination and stories in an area. The most important thing to keep in mind when dealing with the Faery is to take nothing for granted.

Some Faeries move about in troops and are generally sociable, although some are solitary. (The idea of the communal Faeries is traditionally Celtic.) Faeries are divided into two large groups: (1) Those belonging to a Faery race or nation living in the Faery realms in an organized society of their own, such groups as the *side,* that is, people of the hills in Ireland; and (2) The individual Faeries associated with a place, or occupation, or household, such as the undine, a Faery who lives in a spring or stream, the salamander Faery who lives in fire, the buccas in mines, and the brownie who attaches itself to a household.

In his book *Irish Druids and Old Irish Religions,* James Bonwick describes the "Daoine Shee" as examples of a Faery nation or race. Appearing as human beings dressed in green, the Daoine Shee are called "men of peace." Anyone who wants to see them must visit their hill on the eve of Samhain (Halloweve) and walk around their mound nine times counterclockwise. A door will open, revealing the Faery Hosts dancing and playing sweet music. Inviting as it may seem, it is dangerous to accept their hospitality. When you accept their invitation and come in for a dance, you will never again return home.

Santa Claus himself was a "jolly old elf," one of the most familiar types of Faeries. The elves have been molded by contemporary Western culture into Santa's little helpers. Elves prefer natural settings and are frequently found in forests and wooded areas. Usually standing between five and seven feet tall, elves are thin, quick, and amazingly strong, with red, blonde, or light brown hair. Their cat-like eyes are green or blue, and sometimes gold or silver, with slitted pupils, and sometimes they are depicted with cat-like ears as well.

Elves often command other Faery groups and will only respect and befriend mortals who firmly live by their own code and cannot be swayed. Often, elves will attempt to sway such a person and test his or her strength of character before giving friendship. Iron wards off elves and is harmful to them if they touch it, but it does not necessarily kill them. Traditionally, elves are fond of gifts of silver, moonstone, pearl, and quartz.

Elves are closely connected to the magical *cooshie,* or elfin hound. The *cooshie* appears as a large, silver-furred (not white) wolf that moves as fast as a big cat. The *cooshie* does not leave the forest unless its elfin master goes hunting outside the forest, in which case the *cooshie* will accompany him or her. The elfin hound has heightened senses and knows whether there is any magical, spiritual, or physical presence in its territory. Iron can harm the *cooshie,* just as it can elves. Legend tells that *cooshies* have the ability to heal sick or injured travelers and to calm a troubled heart.

Elves are also tied to the *coomlaen,* the elfin steed, which appears as a tall, thin white or silvery horse. The *coomlean* can also be harmed by iron. Living in the forest and always in the company of elves, the *coomlaen* can shape shift, taking any form it desires, but must return to its horse form once a day. Sometimes the elfin steed can be heard nickering in the woods but cannot be seen. The *coomlaen* bonds with one rider at a time and that bond lasts the rider's lifetime. It will defend its rider to the death. To befriend a *coomlaen,* you must first befriend its rider.

Within the elf grouping of Faeries, there are even more groupings of beings. For example, the *Spriggans* are described as the dourest and most ugly set of Faeries belonging to the elfin tribe, who act as a kind of honorary guard to other Faeries. *Spriggans* are seen around old ruins, barrows, giants' quoits and castles, and other places where treasure is buried. *Spriggans* are the ghosts of the old giants. Though usually very small, they can become enormous in size by willing themselves to be so.

The second group of Faeries, which are made up of individuals, are more varied. One of the individual Faery types is the dwarf (not to be confused with human dwarfs). The Faery dwarf is about three to five feet tall with broad shoulders, stumpy limbs, and profuse facial hair. Dwarfs are quick tempered, loyal, and immune to physical damage. They are found underground. In Brittany, dwarfs are thought to haunt the dolmens or ancient graves. Known for mining metals, especially copper and precious gems, dwarfs particularly like gifts of metals and gems.

Like dwarfs, gnomes live underground, and when they appear on the surface (for brief periods only), they remain in the deep forests. Gnomes stand about one to two feet tall, and the males grow long beards. They love gifts of beautiful stones.

One of the more common types of household Faeries is the brownie. They appear in the Scottish Highlands and English folklore and are also found in the Shetland and Western Isles. Wearing a brown cloak and hood, the brownie attaches himself to families and does the chores at night while the people sleep. Milk and cakes are set aside for the brownie, but never any rewards, gifts, or wages, for this will make the brownie depart.

Another familiar household Faery is the *kobold*. *Kobolds* are subterranean Faeries about two feet tall who love to play pranks. Wind and loud noise scare *kobolds* away. This household familiar attaches himself to a human household, where he sleeps on the hearth and is generally helpful, though often playful and mischievous. He does the dishes, sweeps the floor, prepares meals, or makes the fire. He has the ability to cast binding spells and will go to any means to protect the members of the household. A *kobold* needs to be treated with kindness, and food and milk must be left out for him at night. He is usually the size of a small child with the face of an old man, often wearing a cap.

There are many stories of Sidhe women who help households with spinning, housework, and threshing corn. However, if they are interfered with in any way, even by the offering of a present, they will never return again. Alexander Carmichael mentions the *"bean chaol a chot uaine 's na gruaige buidhe,"* the slender woman of the green kirtle and yellow hair, who can turn water into wine and weave spider's webs into plaid, and play sweet music on the Faery reed. The Faery housekeeper is the *bean tighe,* also known as the Glaistig Uaine or Green Lady, who is often sighted in the rooms and the grounds of the old Scottish castles of the ancient clans, watching over everything.

I happened to encounter another kind of Green Lady while walking next to a large oak tree where I live. It was just at dusk, while the last light of the day was fading. It had been raining all day and I was taking advantage of a break in the storm to step outside and get a breath of fresh air. Suddenly, a beautiful lady literally flowed out of the thick trunk of the old oak. She was luminous, with delicate features and long flowing green hair. Her hair seemed to have a life of its own, and streamed freely about her. I wasn't so much frightened of her as awestruck at the size of her, over eight feet tall. I realized that she was a spirit that lived in the tree, referred to as a dryad. She kept looking at me and I kept looking at her. I tried not to move or startle her. I asked her silently who she was, and I got the reply, "I am the Lady of the Tree." She told me how to keep her healthy by trimming some small madrones back to bush-high level, not harming the madrones by doing so, but keeping them from crowding her and spreading disease to her branches. I agreed to do so, and she walked back into the oak tree.

After meeting the Green Lady in the tree, I discovered that dryads, specifically hamadryads, bond to a certain oak tree. Generally, they appear as women, with whorled brown skin and long, wavy, dark green hair. Dryads are friendly, gentle spirits, but they can protect themselves by calling storms and lightning. Once bonded with a tree, the dryad needs the tree in order to survive because the tree provides energy, power, and knowledge. The dryad cannot go far from her tree or she will die. Although there is the rare tale of a dryad moving to another tree if her tree is harmed, generally, once a dryad's tree is cut down, the dryad dies. This is one of the many reasons to stop cutting down trees, groves, and forests, and planting them instead. All trees, in particular, oaks and fruit trees, are physically alive, as well as alive with Faery spirits.

The dryad is commonly classified as a nymph. Some other types of nymphs are the mountain nymphs known as oreads, and the nymphs of streams, wells, springs, and rivers known as naiads. In classical mythology, nymphs were nature spirits who through time developed into the Faeries of general European folklore. They are amoral, amorous, have insatiable sexual appetites, and often take mortal lovers. Nymphs frequently travel in pairs and can move about, sometimes permanently aligning themselves with trees, rock outcroppings, mountains, rivers, and so forth. They appear as young, incredibly beautiful women, dancers, and musicians. According to tradition, a nymph's lifetime was the same as the phoenix, who outlived nine ravens, who outlived three stags, who outlived four crows, and who outlived nine generations of aged mortals. Nymphs have the power of prophecy and are kindly toward humans. They are also said to be extremely hard to avoid once they have taken an interest in you, and they can occasionally be dangerous.

Like the dryad, another kind of Faery is the oakman, who is said to live in oak trees. In the North of England, the oakman is a guardian of the animals. The familiar saying is "Faery folks are in old oaks." In fact, the oak is considered the tree of the dead and the abode of departed spirits. In her book "The Fairy Caravan," Beatrix Potter describes the oakmen as dwarfish folk with red toadstool caps and red noses that live in a thrice-cut copse covered with bluebells.

Other Faeries that dwell in the forests and wooded areas are the pixies and sprites. The pixies generally live closer to mortals and are popular with the Cornish people. They appear as young, tiny humans, about one foot tall. Most pixies and sprites are slender, with blondish hair and green eyes. Sprites usually have long, transparent insect or butterfly-like wings. Both pixies and sprites appear to be excited and agitated. They can be mischievous and levitate small objects. The *sithich* is the most active sprite of Highland mythology. It is a dexterous child-stealer, who is wantonly mischievous. Both pixies and sprites are easily harmed and very fragile.

A distinction is often made between the Sidhe, who are seen walking on the ground after sunset, and the "Sluagh Sidhe," the Faery Host who travel through the air at night and are known to abduct mortals. There are also guardian Sidhe associated with the lakes of Ireland and Scotland. These distinct categories of Sidhe beings tie in with the testimonies of seers who divide the Sidhe into wood spirits, water spirits, and air spirits, that is, the elemental spirits.

The court of the kindly Faery Host is called the "Seelie Court." *Seelie* means "blessed," and these benevolent Faeries give gifts of bread and seed corn to the poor and help to their favorite mortals. In contrast, the "Unseelie Court" is the court of the malevolent Faeries, who are hostile and harmful.

Some Faeries are known to be particularly dangerous, such as the Amadan Dubh, a Sidhe greatly feared among the Gaels. He is the Fairy Fool, bringer of madness and oblivion, and plays a Faery enchantment on his reed pipes on a hillslope after sunset.

Other solitary Faeries considered frightening are the banshees, who are more sociable Faeries grown solitary through much sorrow. The banshee (*bean sidhe*) is probably the most well known of the Faery women. Her name corresponds to the lesser known "Fear Sidhe," or Faery man. The White Lady of Avenel is an example of a banshee, who foretells the death of her descendants. In Ireland the banshee is the ancestress of the old clans, who is more often heard than seen. The banshee wails her unearthly lament when any death or misfortune is about to occur in the family, and she also avenges the deaths of clan members. It is an honor to have a banshee attached to your family. When seen, the banshee is often combing her long hair with a silver comb. The wild banshees are found wandering through the woods, over the moors at dusk, where they lure travelers to their deaths.

Another of the more terrifying Faery women is the *bean nighe*, which is of Scottish origin and is known as the Washer at the Ford. She is seen at midnight washing the death shirt of someone about to die. Usually, she meets the person when he or she is about to die. She sings the person a dirge: *Se do leine, se do leine ga mi nigheadh* ("It is your shirt, your shirt that I am washing").

Perhaps not quite so frightening as the *bean nighe*, but certainly as tormenting, is the boggart. Nearly every old English house had its own boggart. Supernatural and annoying, the boggart is sly, mischievous, and full of tricks but seldom does serious harm. For example, they pull the covers off of sleeping people at night, rap or pound on the door again and again, or rearrange the furniture so that people get up in the night and bump into it. There is an old Lancashire folktale about a farmer who was so annoyed by a boggart he decided to pack up and move to another place. Just as he was explaining why he was moving to his neighbor, he heard an invisible voice speak from inside his loaded wagon. The farmer knew when he was licked, unpacked his things, and decided to remain in his old home with the boggart.

A friendlier being in the Faery realm is the "pooka"

(*phouka*). Similar to the brownie and sometimes a mischievous trickster, the pooka can also be very helpful and well-disposed to mortals and the person or household it attaches itself to. The pooka in Irish legends was often a shape-shifter, who could appear in human or animal form (often a horse) and often lived in lakes and rivers. The ancestral Faery beliefs about the pooka are preserved in places such as Pooka's Ford, Puckstown, Puck Fair, and Carrig-a-Phooka in County Cork.

The Gwyddonic Druid tradition gives specific instructions for creating a pooka. A word of warning: Don't ever fool yourself into thinking you are its master. Pookas can perform many tasks, act as helpful companions, and bring joy to your life. But remember, they are their own creatures, with distinct personal-ities and proclivities.

I suggest you practice the following instructions several times to hone your abilities before actually creating your pooka. Before beginning, decide what you intend to create. Under-stand every detail of your pooka program or formula. A Druid saying goes, "An error in calculation will result in an error in situation." With this in mind, be certain of exactly what qualities you expect in your pooka. Your success rate for creating pookas rests on the strength and clarity of your expectation. You are the creator, and your creation will reflect your abilities.

When first creating your pooka, you need to determine its nature. When doing this, take sufficient time to picture your new energetic being. A question you will need to ask is: How long will the pooka live? The choice between a lifespan of a few moments or a few thousand years gives the creature its tempo-ral character. Decide what tasks it is to complete and determine whether the pooka will be a lifelong companion. If so, choose a special word or phrase that will free it at the time of your death. Your pooka will live on after your physical death for as long as its food supply lasts.

What food will your pooka eat? Your pooka needs to have

some means for renewing its energy, so determine what will act as its basis of nourishment. You can have your pooka live off etheric energy or hydrogen. This would guarantee a viable energy or food source for an extended, perhaps infinite, duration.

Next, define your pooka's form. What does it look like? Does it resemble a wolf, a horse, or perhaps a ball of silver light? Will your pooka be free to move about while resting or will it stay in one place, such as in a ring, statue, or stone? What do you call your new creation? If you give your pooka a name, you can summon it more easily. A name gives your pooka more power. If you have any problems finding your pooka's name, ask it to identify itself.

Decide exactly what duties your pooka is to perform. For example, you may want your pooka to protect you from negative energies, protect your home or car, or bring more wealth into your life. You may want your pooka to help you communicate with other Faery beings, to attract potential mates, or to help you connect with deity. There are no limits to the tasks you can have your pooka perform.

Next, determine where your pooka will live. Be sure to use something that will last the lifetime of the pooka. Pookas are customarily worn or carried on your person. Rings, amulets, and stones make excellent pooka homes. When you make a pooka properly, you create shifts in energy that can play havoc with quartz watches, telephones, and other electronic objects. For that reason, it is not a good idea to use these items for your pooka's home. You may also want to leave a "back door" in the making of your pooka, allowing it to venture out on its own when resting from its duties. By doing so, you give your pooka an opportunity to learn, grow, and evolve.

Pookas most definitely do evolve and develop unique personalities over time. They have either a male or female polarity, and given enough time, pookas can manifest into a tangible form with an individual mind. Your pooka reflects or mirrors you in many ways, absorbing everything that comes in contact with it.

After carefully defining the characteristics and duties of your pooka, you are ready to do the work. Set up your altar as described in chapter 3. Draw your sacred circle and set the Watchtowers in place. Remember to use the Three Eyes of Kerridwen (expectation, desire, and merging) when creating your pooka. Make certain you have a strong desire to successfully create your pooka. Move into a state of mind and a state of being where you want to create your pooka more than anything else. Focus all of your attention and your complete awareness upon creating a new being of light.

Your pooka's abilities and level of power correlate directly to the depth of your merge. As you merge deeply, see and feel yourself taking a portion (like a sphere or ball) of unmanifested energy. Shape this energy with your mind and hands, into the pooka you have outlined previously. The best way to do this is to stand in front of a mirror and see the sphere of unmanifest energy as a shining ball of energy. Hold the ball of energy between your hands and mold it, concentrating on shaping it with your intention into your predetermined specifications.

If you find you make an error in the procedure, release the pooka and try again. To release your pooka from its relationship with you, simply merge again as deeply as when you originally created it and let the pooka go. Keep working with these techniques until you feel comfortable with them.

Faeries and Mortals

Keeping promises and fair dealing are mortal virtues respected and often rewarded by the Faeries, as are the abilities to keep Faery secrets and guard against any intrusions upon the privacy of the Faeries in order to preserve their traditional way of life.

Gentleness and politeness are assets when communicating with the Faeries, as are being open, capable of generosity, and ready to share with anyone in need; however, boasting and bragging are unpopular.

From time to time, mention is made of the Faeries' dependence on mortals. For example, Faeries eat mortal food and are known for taking grain, milk, and butter. Another example is the Faeries' need, now and again, for mortal midwives to assist them in childbirth. Sometimes young women are stolen as Faery brides, giving the impression that mortal blood is needed to strengthen the Faery race.

Faeries often mingle in the affairs of mortals. The six types of relationships of Faeries to mortals are as follows:

1. Mortal visits to the Faery realm.
2. Faeries assist and help mortals.
3. The Faery lover.
4. Changelings.
5. Faeries abduct mortals for a specific reason.
6. Faeries harm mortals.

Several dramatic accounts of mortals visiting the "dim" world of the Faery realm by accident or invitation abound in folklore. Mortals are frequently lured by Faery music. Hearing the sweet and beautiful music of the Faeries, they follow it to the Faery realm. A well-known authority on the fairies, W. B. Yeats writes in his book *Fairy and Folk Tales of Ireland:*

> Many more have listened to their fairy music, till all human cares and joys drifted from their hearts and they became great peasant seers or "Fairy Doctor," or great peasant musicians or poets like Carolan, who gathered his tunes while sleeping on a fairy rath; or else they died in a year and a day, to live every after among the fairies.

One boy went and danced with the Faery throng and his brother brought him safely out. He thought he had been dancing for a few minutes, but actually he had been gone for over a year.

Faeries help in the field with planting and harvesting, cutting wood, and herding animals. The *gruagach* is a Faery woman who watches over the cattle at night and protects the goodness of the milk. On Skye, Tiree, and other islands are "*gruagach* stones." These stones have hollows where libations of milk were poured as an offering to her. Faeries are also known to rescue damsels in distress and give gifts of gold, gossamer cloth, and vessels that always remain full of food or grain.

Fertility, true love, and the comings and goings of lovers are always under Faery patronage. By far, the most mysterious and poetic of all stories of the Faery are those of the Faery lover or mistress, where the union of a Faery and a mortal follow a fixed pattern. A mortal loves a Faery and the Faery consents to marry the mortal on one condition. Frequently, the mortal breaks the condition and loses the Faery lover, and sometimes tries to recover the lover and often succeeds.

In the Faery lover stories, sometimes there is a complication in the union of Faery and mortal; the mortal finally wants to return home and is permitted to do so, only to discover that he has been away a very long time. These stories end with the mortal turning old suddenly and then into dust.

Yeats describes the *Leanhaun sidhe,* or Faery mistress, as a spirit that seeks the love of mortal men. If the mortal refuses, she is theirs; if they consent, they are hers and can escape only by finding someone to take their place. Because she lives on their life energy, her mortal lovers waste away. Yeats writes:

> Most of the Gaelic poets, down to quite recent times, have had a Leanhaun Shee, for she gives inspiration to her slaves and is indeed the Gaelic muse—this malignant fairy. Her

lovers, the Gaelic poets, died young. She grew restless and carried them away to other worlds, for death does not destroy her power.

It's no wonder some Faeries, in particular the Merrow women, prefer handsome mortal fishermen to their green-haired, green-toothed Faery lovers with pigs' eyes and red noses. Near Bantry, in the eighteenth century, there was a woman covered with scales like a fish, who was the offspring of just such a union.

The "Ganconer," or "Gean-canogh," is a leprachaun-type Faery who also prefers mortal lovers. He is called the love-talker and always appears in lonely valleys and fields with a pipe in his mouth, spending most of his time making love to mortal milkmaids and shepherdesses.

In the contemporary Faery tradition, the concept of the Faery lover or mistress has evolved. Now, when you work with a Faery ally, there is a sexual connection, but it is an equal exchange of energies, not one that gives it or you personal selfish gratification. After all, spirits do materialize and mortals have seen them eating food, drinking tea, and moving objects. Many people have been touched by spirits. In this light, the concept of a Faery lover or marriage with a male or female spirit may not be so far-fetched.

Changelings (*corpan side* or *siodbrad*) are Faeries, sometimes one or two thousand years old, left in the place of newborn infants. Generally, the Faery child rejoins its own folk in the Faery realm. Many methods are used to keep the Faery from abducting mortal children. Certain objects placed next to the child were believed to be effective, such as knives, scissors, rowan plants, and garlic. When changelings grow up with mortals, they are beautiful of face and endowed with extraordinary abilities.

There are many stories of Faeries abducting adult mortal

women and men, taking them to the Faery realm and casting spells on humans. When midwives are abducted to help Faery mothers in childbirth, they are blindfolded to and from the Faery realm and handsomely rewarded for their services.

Some Faeries harm the crops, milk animals in the field, ride horses in the night, blow out the candles in the house, knock things off shelves, send gusts of smoke down the chimney, and prevent the fire from lighting. Sometimes the pranks are ways of punishing mortals. Some Faeries cast binding spells on mortals and hinder and hound them at every opportunity as a form of punishment for rudeness or harm done to one of them.

Other stories tell of the Faeries helping mortals and receiving gifts for their help. Faeries like apples, wine, berries, nuts, milk, butter, flour, cakes, corn, and whisky. Traditionally, a little food is left out for the Faeries overnight. The food is made without any salt because Faeries do not like salt. Faeries are especially fond of milk, and any leftover milk is customarily poured on the ground for them. Some farmers leave one cow in their herd for the Faeries to milk.

The Faeries also had their own herds of milk-white cattle, called the "Gwartheg y Llyn." In Wales, these cattle were given as part of the dowry of a Lake Maiden (Gwragedd Annwn). Sometimes one of the Faery water-bulls would visit an earthly herd, with fortunate results to the owner. A stray Faery cow once attached herself to an earthly bull. The owner of the bull became the richest farmer in the countryside, with prize calves and the best milk and cheese that could be found.

Years went by and the farmer became more and more greedy and arrogant. One day he decided it was time to fatten the Faery cow for market. His neighbors assembled to see the death of the famous Faery cow. Just as the butcher raised his knife, his arm become paralyzed and the knife dropped out of his hand. A sharp cry rang out and a tall Faery woman clad in green stood on the crag above the Llyn. She sang out, calling her Faery cattle home. The fattened Faery cow broke loose and ran up the mountain to the Faery woman and was followed by all of her offspring. The Faery woman then led her cattle into the dark waters of the lake, leaving a cluster of yellow water lilies to mark the spot where they sank into the lake.

Faery cattle were not the only domesticated animals of the Faery realm to disappear into a lake. The last of the Faery horses of the Tuatha De Danann also disappeared in this manner. Lady Wilde in her book *Ancient Legends of Ireland,* describes the horses of the Tuatha as being swift as the wind, broad-chested with finely arched necks and quivering nostrils, and large eyes that blazed with fire. Their bridles were of gold, their shoes silver, and they were stabled in large caves in the hills. Some of these magical horses lived for centuries by their enchantments and were so well-known that they were often commonly seen and identified by the Irish people (and still are).

The last of these splendid Tuatha De Danann horses belonged to a great lord in Connaught. When the lord died, the royal steed was auctioned off to an Englishman who wanted to breed the horse. When they were transporting the horse, a groom tried to mount the Faery steed and was thrown and killed immediately. The magical horse galloped away and then dove into the lake and was never seen again. So ended the line of the Tuatha De Danann horses in Ireland.

Faery Queens

The realm of the Faery is populated in great numbers and ruled over by a queen and king. Generally, the queen is the leader of the two. Known as *bean righean na brugh,* the Faery Queen of the palace, these queens are the Goddesses of local tribes. Many are still said to be the guardians of Irish clans.

The Faery Queens and Kings are indeed the old pagan Gods and Goddesses "in disguise" who have long been revered by the

Irish. Some say the Celtic pagan Goddesses and Gods have long disappeared and have been replaced by Catholicism and Christianity. But everyone who has visited Ireland and has listened to the local stories and folk tales can tell that the pagan Goddesses and Gods are still very much alive. They live on in such folk tales as the giants of the hill, the Gobhan Saor who built all the bridges of Ireland, and the Gille Decair, a trickster.

Certain locals are more strongly influenced by Faery energies than others. For example, three miles southwest of Lough Gur in County Limerick is Knockainy or Cnoc Aine, the hill of Aine, one of the strongholds of the popular Faery Queen of Munster who is honored throughout Ireland. Daughter of the Druid Owel, Aine was a mortal woman who was "taken" by the Fae. Every year on Midsummer's Eve, people go in a procession around the hill of Aine and then carry flaming torches through the crop fields. Some say Aine herself was seen on many occasions leading the procession. She is still associated with the fertility observances on Cnoc Aine on Midsummer Eve.

In County Louth, Aine can be found at Dunany point (Dun Aine). Each year, the first Friday, Saturday, and Sunday after Lughnassad are dedicated to her. During these three days, Aine claims a life.

Many families in Great Britain, especially Ireland, claim to be decendants of the Fae. For example, the O'Corra family in County Derry are Aine's decendants. The O'Briens who are the decendants of Brian Boru, claim that Aoibheal, the Faery Queen who rules from Craig Liath in County Clare, is their ancestral deity. Aoibheal tried to protect her people by forewarning them of the outcome at the Battle of Clontarf. This is a common theme with the Fae, that of helping those mortals they protect and love.

In fact, many of the Sidhe queens and kings are known to have encounters or relationships with mortals. For example, the Earl of Desmond spotted the Faery Queen Aine combing her hair while she sat on the banks of a river. Upon seeing her, he fell madly in love with her, seized her Faery cloak, and married her. Their enchanted son Gerald, fourth Earl of Desmond, lives today under the deep waters of Lock Gur. Reappearing once every seven years, he rises up above the surface of the water riding a shining white horse. Munster families still claim descent from him.

Cliodna of the Fair Hair is one of the three great Faery Queens of Munster and a master shape-shifter. She was once an Irish princess, then a Munster Goddess, and now a Faery Queen. She is known to take mortal lovers and is reputed to be a sensuous and powerful seducer of young spirited men, especially at fairs on May Day. Cliodna's name means "shapely one," and she becomes the most beautiful of all women when she takes human form. Eldest daughter of Gebann, chief Druid to Manannan, Cliodna is loved and cherished by the people of County Cork, where a number of places are associated with her. She is the guardian Goddess of the O'Keefes and also believed to be the special banshee of families in the south of Munster.

Her mortal lover, Ciaban of the Curling Locks, was carried by a rider on a grey horse that rose out of the sea, to Tir Tairngaire, the Land of Promise and the city of Manannan. A great feast was going on when he arrived, and the guests were challenged to throw nine straight willow rods into the rafters of the house and catch them coming down, while standing on one leg and with one hand behind their back. Ciaban was handed the nine rods and he successfully performed the trick. Cliodna loved Ciaban from that moment and went away with him the next morning. They left in a curragh to the south shore of Ireland. Ciaban anchored the boat on the strand and went hunting for food. Cliodna stayed behind with Iuchna, one of Manannan's musicians that came with them. Iuchna played magical music that put Cliodna to sleep. While she slept, Manannan sent a huge wave rolling over the strand and the curragh, drowning Cliodna and sweeping her away to sea. That place, just off the coast at Glandore, County Cork, is still called Tonn

Cliodna, or Cliodna's Wave, and it is believed that Cliodna will always rule the ninth wave of every series.

Grainne of the Bright Cheeks is the popular Faery Queen in the northeast of Leinster and has her home on Cnoc Greine. In the Finn cycle of Irish heroic story and romance, she is the strong-willed daughter of Cormac mac Art, who fell in love with Diarmuid after being promised by her father to the hero Finn MacCool. On Diarmuid's forehead was a magical love spot, and when Grainne saw it, she fell helplessly in love with him. In the Irish sagas, Grainne persuaded Diarmaid to run away and elope with her. Across Ireland, where the lovers traveled and slept in rocky alcoves, there are cairns and cromlechs still known as the beds of Diarmuid and Grainne.

Faery Kings

King of the dead in County Galway in the west of Ireland and the King of the Faeries in Connacht is Finnbeara (Finnvarra). He dwells in Cnoc Meadha, a prominent hill west of Tuam. On top of the hill is a burial mound. By his presence in Cnoc Meadha, the crops of the region are abundant, but when Finnbeara is away, the harvest is lean.

Finnbeara is more powerful than any mortal man and the stories about him continue to this day. He is known to love horses and is often seen riding a black horse with flaring red nostrils. Sometimes he invites young mortal men to ride with his Faery Host. One story tells of Finnbeara paying a smith a pound note because the smith was not afraid to shoe Finnbeara's three-legged horse. The Faery King, completely in character, delivered the pound note on a puff of wind.

There are many stories of Finnbeara taking mortal women as lovers. He would often lure young girls away to dance all night with him in his palace in Cnoc Meadha, but the next morning they were always found safely asleep in bed. One lord, whose home was close to Cnoc Meadha, was not so fortunate. Ethna, his bride, the most beautiful woman in Ireland, was taken by Finnbeara. While Ethna was dancing one evening, shining like moonlight in her silver dress at a great ball, her hand slipped from her partner's and she fell to the ground in a swoon. When she was revived, she spoke of an Otherworld she had visited, to which she desperately wanted to return.

The next night Ethna fell asleep under the close guard of her old nurse, but in the quiet of the night, her nurse also fell asleep. The next morning Ethna was gone. The lord knew that Finnbeara had taken his bride and started to dig down into Cnoc Meadha, but during the night, while the lord and his workers slept, the Faeries filled in the deep cleft with earth, covering the area with grass as if it had never been disturbed. More diggers were hired the second and third days, and they dug down even farther into the Faery mound, but again, as they slept, the cleft was filled back in and covered with turf. On the third night, the lord was told to sprinkle the dug out area with salt and to place a line of burning turf around the deep cleft. The lord did as he was instructed and the next morning the digging was left untouched.

Finnbeara came out of the Faery mound, as he knew that if one human spade cut into his palace wall, his home would crumble to dust. The Faery King told the mortal men to lay down their spades and that at sunset he would return Ethna to her husband.

At sunset the lord rode to the mouth of the glen and the beautiful Ethna walked up to him through the deep cleft, shining like silver. He drew her up to his horse's back and they returned home, but Ethna was in a trance and nothing would rouse her.

One night, the lord was riding home and heard a voice tell him that it had been a year and a day since Ethna had returned from the realm of the Faeries and that Finnbeara still had possession of his bride's soul in Cnoc Meadha. In order to win her back to mortal life, he was told he had to undo the girdle around her waist and take out the Faery pin with which it was fastened. Then he had to burn the girdle and sprinkle the ashes outside Ethna's door and bury the Faery pin in the earth. He did this and took the Faery pin and buried it under a Faery thorn where it would not be disturbed. He returned to Ethna's side. She suddenly knew and remembered everything except that the time she had spent in the Faery realm seemed like only a night to her. The deep cleft is still in Cnoc Meada and is called Fairy Glen.

Another king of the dead is the Faery King Donn of Knock-fierna in County Limerick. Donn is the name of the ancient Celtic God of Death who rules the rocky islands to the south-west on Ireland's Atlantic coast and who now resembles a medieval landlord rather than a God. Donn is also claimed as an ancestor by the Maguires, whom he helped in battle.

At Donn's home, located on one of the small islands off southwest Munster, the dead gather just before their journey to the Otherworld and the Isles of the Blessed. There is a large earthen fort and several dolmens called the "Giants Graves" on Donn's hill and you can see the threshold to his Faery kingdom. On stormy nights when he is seen riding on his shining white horse, people say that Donn is galloping in the clouds.

The Faery Tradition

The Faery tradition may be one of the oldest traditions prac-ticed by humankind. Not only a living Celtic tradition, the Faery tradition is also Norse, Germanic, Finnish, Lapp, and Lithuan-ian. Visionary and poetic, the Faery tradition inspires your inherent spiritual vision and expression, showing you how to attune to the sacred land and in the process align yourself with the elements and seasonal changes.

The Faery tradition encourages you to journey to the other-worlds of the Faery, to see through their eyes, to feel the sensations they experience, and to hear what they hear. In turn, they look through your eyes, hear through your ears, and touch with your hands. One of the ways to access this rapport experience with the Faery is to commune with one of your ancestors. This is done by merging with a photograph of your ancestor. Do this at night during the full moon. First, light two small white taper candles in candle holders, and then place the photo in a position where the candlelight shines clearly on its face. If you are working inside, dim the lights in the room. Now focus all of your attention on the photo for a few minutes. Breathe deeply and rhythmically all the while you are focusing on the photo, by breathing in to the count of three, holding your breath for three counts, and then exhaling completely to the count of three. Become one with the photo and every aspect of your ancestor's face, body, persona. Chant: *I am* (name of ancestor), (name of ancestor) *is me, we are one*. Do this repetitively for about three minutes. Then close your eyes and merge completely with the intention of becoming one with your ancestor for a few moments or hours. Do this by allowing yourself, your mind, your entire being to become one with all things—the photo, your ancestor, the candles, the candle flames, your breathing, any noises outside, the moon, the night sky, the universe—everything. Rather than focusing your attention on any one thing, just let your mind become diffused like a cloud. Meditate or sit quietly while the candles burn all the way down, mentally noting or writing down any impressions that come to you.

Another way to exchange worlds with the Faery is to develop a relationship with an individual Faery such as a dryad, lake maiden, Faery King, or Faery Queen. This kind of experience can lead to perceptional expansion and a clearer understanding of dimensional awareness.

Your body is one of the best vessels of magical energy. You

don't need any special tools or artifacts to access the Underworld of the Faery, only your ability to merge with Oneness.
Through conscious intent and merging with Oneness, you have
the ability to create morphogenic fields capable of influencing
change. You are the linking being between the Underworld and
the mortal world. Due to genetic memory, a great part of our
being always exists in the Underworld.

The Faery truth is that all living creatures are interwoven,
living upon and within one another. All things are one, whatsoever they may be, and everything is made of the same stellar
stuff, from starseed. Your physical body is halfway between the
mortal world and the Otherworld, somewhere between instinct
and spirit. Parts of yourself exist within the very body of the
planet, in the Sun, and the stars. What you begin to understand
as you come to this realization is that to be a complete being,
you need to learn to integrate your mortal and Faery aspects
into one.

Celtic magical traditions have been kept alive orally in Celtic
poems, epics, songs, stories, and Faerytales. The stories are keys
to ancestral wisdom and to accessing and renewing the sacred
power of the land. The oral tradition, passed down for generations, preserves the knowledge for communicating with deities,
using magical energies, and learning how to connect with other
realms of existence within the Earth, such as the Faery realm.
Fortunately, the ancient magical traditions, such as the Faery
tradition, are now gaining the recognition they deserve, as vital
and productive ways for balancing a world dangerously out of
balance.

Dreaming of the Underworld of the Faeries

Dreaming is one avenue to a deeper understanding of the Faery
realm and the Underworld. Dream is a vehicle for the cosmic
mind of Oneness and acts as a symbolic dimension of human

experience as a whole. Interestingly, mirror worlds and all sorts of Otherworlds, such as the Underworld of the Faery, are commonly experienced in dream.

Stemming from your inner core, dreams are the expressions of experiences seeking to become real in the future on some level. If you can dream of an experience, you can manifest it into tangible reality. Because dreams are a source of tremendous creativity, they are the perfect place to begin a further understanding of, and thus interact with, the realm of the Faery.

Like other altered states of consciousness, dreaming allows your conscious mind to actively participate in processes that are normally considered unconscious. Dreams allow you to enter that otherworldly threshold between here and there, now and then, and the mortal and Faery. In dream there exists a continuous communication between all parts of yourself, and this can be used to enhance your ability to enter, and move about in, other dimensions of awareness.

Many dreams have a message that can help you see something you haven't yet grasped with your conscious mind, such as otherworldly experiences. Also, your dreams and bodily responses give you a chance to explore your inner processes. They display parts of the world you can learn to recognize inside yourself and in others. From your dreams spring the possibilities of experience, whatever they may be.

As you learn to direct your dreams through conscious intent, dreaming shifts into a multidimensional experience. The alchemy of the spirit is to become multidimensional, simultaneously being one with all things. Separating ordinary reality from multidimensional reality, waking reality from the dream state, as well as time from space, or white from black doesn't make much sense and seems to be an obsolete view, particularly as you live in a world where everything is gray.

As you practice dreaming and merging, you begin to view time differently. While learning that time has circular, horizontal, and vertical qualities, you also begin to have many viewpoints simultaneously and seem to be connected to Otherworlds, rather than your Earthly reality.

As time and space take on more infinite qualities, the false structures and the distractions that keep you from Oneness start to crumble. Some of these false structures include television, radio, newspapers, five-day work weeks, weekends, clocks, calendars, schools, garbage collection, mail delivery, and anything else that fools you into thinking that its time and space structure or form is "real." Metaphysically speaking, when you learn to travel beyond the time and space continuum, form and structure become agreed-upon concepts within the continuum and are subject to change at any moment. Once you grasp this fact, visiting the Faery realm seems less unreal and more real than you would have ever imagined.

Underworld Journeys

The reason that children hear and see the Faeries more often than adults may be because it is always best to be pure of heart, open-minded, honest, and steadfast of will when journeying to the Underworld of the Faery. Entering the Faery realms involves intentionally stepping between the mortal and Faery worlds. This is called "walking between worlds" or "twinkling" and frequently includes physical translation into other realms, and hopefully the subsequent physical return to the mortal world. I prefer taking experiential journeys to the Underworld where I take my energetic body with me rather than my physical body.

The Underworld of the Faery is alive in folklore. For example, in a folk story from northwestern Wales, a householder makes the acquaintance of one of the "Tylwyth Teg," the Fair People, one of the Other Ones. When he says he would like to see the homeland of the Other Ones, a realm normally invisible to mortals, he is invited to place his foot on top of the Faery's. By virtue of the contact of mortal and Faery, suddenly a world is revealed in a chasm in the ground before him, with fertile fields, crowded roads, marketplaces, and homes, a land with gleaming rivers twisting to the sea.

The Underworld, like all things, is made of energy. Mortals, Faeries, Goddesses, and Gods are aspects of energy. They represent the many shapes, clusters, and fields of creative energies that exist within the many dimensions along the continuum. Some Faeries, like mortals, are particularly helpful, and they will literally light your path. Some are not helpful and seek to harm you. Using your intuition and experience will help you know which beings to communicate and connect with. As you interact in the Faery dimension, keep in mind that it's all energy, and energy can be shaped and patterned. Energetic form shifts shape as you shift your attention.

Underworld experiences liberate and unify your energies and perceptions rather than rationalize and separate them. Your perception of yourself in the Faery realm is much different than it is in the mortal realm. The Underworld of the Faery embodies the planetary mind of Mother Earth. The deeper you delve into the Underworld of the Faery, the closer you come to touching the light within the Earth, what R. J. Stewart calls "the power within the land." To the Celts, the light within the earth was that of spirit living within matter.

The Underworld harbors hidden secrets. There are many tales of places you can only glimpse by moonlight, places that have long disappeared, remaining only in folklore and the living traditions. The Underworld can be a wellspring of spiritual wisdom and ancestral lore, representing a world where mortals and Faeries, both visible and invisible, can communicate and interact. Some Faery links are created through intent and others through genetic memory. All links are forever connections.

When you journey to the Underworld, you step into a kind of

timeless present or eternal now. There is emphasis on ancestors and Faeries, but as you evolve, you begin to move into a
timeless awareness that takes you from tribal, to collective, to
universal, and finally to cosmic. Something actually changes in
your awareness of dimensional reality.

Understanding the Underworld creates a conscious relationship between the land, Faeries, mortals, and the Mother Earth.
The Faery tradition is a way of relating, a way of translating
between the mortal and Faery, between the physical and spiritual. As R. J. Stewart writes in *The Living World of Faery:*

> By this deep art one may reach through pools, enter hills and
> trees, meld with stones, and come at last to the halls of the
> People of Light, who are within the body of the Land. And
> they may also come to you, for the threshold once opened
> may be crossed in either direction. You may see with their
> eyes and they likewise shall see with yours for mutual learning.

After journeying into the Faery realm and while visiting this
Underworld, you may experience an enhancement of your
normal vision. This enhancement can be brought into your
mortal realm as well. You perceive the mortal world in a different way. You experience a shifting of your consciousness. When
you work with the Faery and you see through each other's eyes,
you suddenly see the mortal world as the Faery sees it, and they
see the Faery world as you see it. Through this relationship, you
radically change the way you view your physical world. This
becomes a permanent shift of awareness.

Each time I have journeyed into the Underworld, I have met
extraordinary beings of all sizes, seldom anyone under four feet
tall. These folk have many shades of skin, mostly earthen colors,
and all manner and color of eyes. Very few of these beings have
been ghostlike but instead mostly seemed to be flowing, gentle,
wise, and sometimes exotic and to have the ability to travel from
point A to point B in a single thought. Many times I have been

given gifts of knowledge and inspiration, and occasionally I am asked to do certain tasks to aid the Faery realm.

What I have discovered from my Underworld experiences is that the Faeries are always present; it's just that I'm not always present with them. What I have also discovered is that you are interacting with these beings, these energies, and these dimensions of existence all of the time, in a kind of timeless exchange, whether or not you are aware of it.

Example of an Underworld Dream

The following is an example of an Underworld dream I had that I would like to share with you:

> I feel myself moving down through the base of a tree trunk, through the darkness where there is no sensation, to the place far below the roots of the tree. I am in a room hollowed out of earth, somewhere in the Otherworld. It feels like I am underground. The light is dim, golden, but very warm. The walls are earthen. There is a man with a domino-shaped amethyst, but about twice the size of an ordinary domino. He is conducting a game several beings are playing, including myself. We are all standing around a table made of wood or earth, something with a very natural feel to it. The table has a glossy surface.
>
> The game master is thin and tall (over six feet) and looks about forty, with longish brown-blond hair pulled back. He has a gold-brown poet's shirt on. The arms of the shirt are full and billowy, with no buttons in front, and a high collar. There is some sort of insignia on the front of his shirt, almost like Theban letters, roundish and long. The letters obviously mean something. There are two such letter-symbols, embroidered in darker gold-brown on the chest of his shirt. The letter-symbol on top is larger than the one on bottom and the combination of them looks a lot like a crop circle. He also wears tight dark brown pants and bark brown boots.

I am standing next to the game master, facing the table. Suddenly the game master turns to me, and he hands me the crystal and says, "Do what you need to do." I realize I am supposed to activate the amethyst-colored stone for the game. What is more surprising to me while in the dream is that I actually know how to do this. I take the stone in my hands. It feels warm and then hot. The heat radiating from my hands activates a white band of light around the center of it. The band looks like a white stripe of light. I pass the stone back to the game master. He holds it for a moment and then casts it, hard, across the glossy surface of the table as if it were a die. The stone becomes alive and starts moving and dancing over the table after he tosses it on the surface. I am awed at how the stone can be tossed onto the hard glossy surface of the table without damaging or chipping the stone or the table surface.

The game master smiles to a little man standing on my right. The little man is no more than four and a half feet tall and has a full beard, has lots of hair, and is dressed completely in brown. He has a huge smile on his face as his eyes follow the stone dancing across the table. The game master says to him, "Now aren't you glad you came tonight, Coyote?" The little man grins and nods his head.

Guided Journey to the Underworld of the Faery

Follow along now as I take you on a guided journey to the Underworld of the Faery.

Make an effort, even if briefly, to enter the Underworld of the Faery. See and sense yourself moving through the story slowly, mirroring the experiences and actions of the first person "I."

I feel the coarseness of the oak tree's bark under my hands and feet. The moment my skin makes contact with the tree, a chasm abruptly appears in the ground at the foot of the oak, opening into a different reality—an Underworld. There are strange yet familiar people in this Underworld, fertile fields, gleaming rivers twisting to the seas, as well as magical forests and dwellings.

Climbing down the large tree in the darkness of the day, I carefully crawl into the chasm and down a long, steep, winding passageway. Moving to the end of the passageway, I find myself at the edge of a bright, sun-filled village. I sit for a time under a large oak that stands guard at the entrance to the small village, pondering this strange Underworld. Strange lights fill the sky now and again, and a mysterious wind flips across the land, through the foliage of the forest and over my skin.

I stare hypnotized by the dancing shadows of the tree as they play upon the ground and across my legs and feet. I watch as the shapes of the jagged oak leaves, their shadows dark upon the grass, dart to and fro like a band of unruly elves. In their chaotic procession, they cross and whirl and then rest until the next breath of the wind carries them away.

The shadow-tree in all its splendor washes over me like a cool wave and I feel its movement and its dark form upon my arms and shoulders. I sense more of the tree in its shadowed essence on the ground and on my body than when I look directly upon the tree itself. The tree seems to take on deeper qualities in its shadow, as if its shadow were its true form. In the darkness, all that is forever hidden is revealed. Fine threads of light shimmer from the shadows of the leaves, crisscrossing each other and weaving my awareness into their pattern. In the fine lattice of light, I discover the place between the image of the tree and its shadow, and in this place of dream and wonder, I merge my Mind with the boundless oak.

Suddenly everything seems filled with the curious stillness of a dream world. In the next moment, the tree mindspeaks to me through the contact of bark with flesh, her voice soft and nurturing: "My shadow expresses the changes in me at the fluttering of a breeze, and just as my shadow has no permanent pattern, the same is true of me. We are all forever-changing, forever-growing and forever-flowing." As her syllables meld into my thoughts, something nameless within me awakens.

She gently mindspeaks her name to me as if to a child, "My name is Celyn. I am tenanted by the spirit and light of the first ancestor of the village. My health mirrors the people's health." The oak mindspeaks again, "I rule their destiny as the spirit of the ancestor tree. I control the weather, make the sun shine, and cause the people and animals to multiply and prosper." Her silent words grow louder as the wind blows through her boughs.

Suddenly, at the base of the giant oak, Celyn steps out of the very roots of the tree and stands before me. Her skin shines a pale white and her eyes a deep emerald green. Her hair flows down to her feet, a dark forest green. She wears transparent gossamer robes and seems ageless, neither young nor old. Her body glows with a luminous green fire, and as she moves toward me, she holds my light force in the palm of her left hand. Dense trefoils of white-green light flow all around her and the ancestor tree without consuming them. Instead, the green fire connects woman and tree together into one as I watch her metamorphosis.

Celyn beckons me through a large cleft in the oak tree, and with her left hand she offers my light force to me. I feel the brilliance spill into me from her hand and stare in awe at the power of the Lady. She guides me away from the tree and into a thick forest that surrounds the village. "Come, we must hurry. So quickly bright things come to confusion," she mindspeaks, taking me by the hand. Her touch feels like the touch of the greenery of the forest; cool and damp as though it could quench one's thirst.

The ground feels spongy under my feet, cushioned by leaves, needles, and grasses. The Underworld forest smells of water, wildflowers, trees, and damp grass. Celyn leads me to a clearing surrounded by nine large oaks. A small stream borders the clearing and its steady movement sounds like liquid crystal flowing over the rocky terrain. Three large menhirs, carved with cup and ring markings, rise up in front of the thick branches of the grove of trees.

The Lady, glowing with white-green fire, takes a star-tipped stick out from the folds of her diaphanous robe. She hands it to me briefly and I feel it vibrate strangely in my hands. It seems both crafted and living.

"This wand is of stellar origin, given to me by the seven sisters long ago. Within its tip rests a piece of Starseed," Celyn's mind merges with mine as she describes the tool while I finger its intricate carved design.

"This wand has the Star Knowledge, the wisdom of stars before the birth of Earth, of the stars within the very land itself."

Taking the wand back, she uses it to draw a circle of blue-white light around the clearing. The shimmering circle spirals in constant motion, clockwise toward the center again and again. She knocks the end of the wand nine times on the oak nearest her, in three sets of three. The tree sings back to her in the gentle wind and then a large opening appears at the base of the tree, large enough for someone to enter.

Celyn beckons for me to enter and takes my hand. As we move through the opening, I see a magical garden filled with every kind of blooming flower. A large pool of clear water rests at the center of the garden. Celyn takes me over to the pool, dips her hand into the water, and strokes my eyes with her moist fingers. As she does this, she silently says, "Now you will always be able to see me clearly whenever you choose." I take a white petal gently from a nearby rose and hand it to Celyn and think to her, "This is a token of my eternal love." We sit silently by the pool for what seems to be hours and when I look around me, the light is like twilight.

I look upward and gasp as I see a large serpent-like dragon flying straight for us, its crests strangely gleaming in the twilight, shining with all of the colors of the rainbow. The dragon's wings look like the feathers of a peacock's tail, awash with color. I point upward excitedly, but Celyn just smiles and waits quietly for the dragon to glide down, sparkling all over, and settle upon the ground on the opposite side of the pool. The dragon shimmers as it folds its wings and begins to drink from the pool.

Celyn spreads her hands outward toward the red dragon in a gesture of welcome, and the dragon stops drinking for a moment, looking straight at us, and then continues drinking in the next moment. Celyn mindspeaks to me, "There are energies of creativity and destruction that flow from this land to the lands above and below. They flow through me and you, through the very body of the land, bringing the power of prophecy and second sight. The dragon embodies these energies." She knocks three times on the ground next to her with the star-tipped wand and just as suddenly as we entered the garden, we are transported back to the edge of the bright, sun-filled village. We stand next to the large oak that guards the entrance to the small village, Celyn's tree. She touches my forehead, smiles, and then turns and touches the trunk of the oak with her wand, flowing effortlessly into the tree.

I find myself moving slowly up the dark passageway into the mortal world, feeling the bark of the tree against my skin once again.

5

CODERN CELTIC TRADITIONS

We shall be notes in that great Symphony
Whose cadence circles through the rhythmic spheres,
And all the live World's throbbing heart shall be
One with our heart; the stealthy creeping years
Have lost their terrors now, we shall not die,
The Universe itself shall be our Immortality.

From the poem "Panthea" by Oscar Wilde

Celtic Pagan Traditions

Over the past three thousand years, the Celtic people have kept the mystery traditions of Europe alive for everyone, traditions that remain more relevant and applicable than most others in our modern times. The majority of Celtic pagan practices and traditions have their roots in Celtic spirituality and mythology, stemming from pre-Christian European mystery traditions. Contrary to what some scholars claim, the majority of these are revivals and offshoots of the ancient mysteries, albeit some are fabrications or modern reconstructions.

Celtic pagan traditions derive from the Old Religion or Goddess Religion of antiquity. This becomes patently clear when
you are initiated and become part of a Celtic mystery tradition
such as the Welsh Druidic tradition I am familiar with, called
Gwyddonic Druid tradition. Unfortunately, many of those who
falsely claim that Celtic pagan traditions lack authenticity are
those who intellectually study Western magical traditions but
have never experienced initiation, ritual, shamanic states of consciousness, or divine rapport firsthand.

Celtic traditions were influenced by the many cultures the
Celts encountered throughout history. Accordingly, Celtic pagan
traditions such as Wicca have become a melting pot of spiritu-
alities such as Druidism, the living tradition of the Faery, folk
traditions, and witchcraft, much like the United States is a melting pot of many races of peoples. This is probably one of the
reasons Celtic pagan traditions are so popular and still growing
strong in America.

Modern Celtic Paths

The word *Celtic* covers a lot of the traditions practiced today,
which are basically variations on a common theme. Following is
a list of many of the modern Celtic-based or Celtic-influenced
magical traditions. More paths constantly stem from these,
which is consistent with Celtic philosophy and its independent
streak.

Anglo-Romany Tradition   Based on the beliefs of "Tinkers," the
Gypsy people of Britain and Ireland.

Anglo-Saxon Tradition   An English path combining the practice
of the Celts with those of the southern Teutons.

Ar nDraiocht Fein (ADF)   Popular Druid tradition with three
worlds, gates, and a primary focus on the grove.

Arthurian Tradition   A tradition from Wales and Cornwall based
upon the Arthurian myths.

Brezonek Tradition   Celtic tradition of Brittany.

Brittanic Tradition   An Anglo-Celtic tradition that blends Roman and Celtic beliefs.

Brythonic Traditions   Common name of traditions of Wales, Cornwall, and England.

Caledonii Tradition   Scottish tradition with Roman influences.

Celtic Tradition   Catch-all term used to designate paganism originating in Wales, Scotland, Brittany, the Isle of Man, northern and western England, and Celtic Gaul. Common and different elements exist within the tradition.

Celtic Wicca   One of the most popular magical traditions in America. Prefers couples working together and focusing on ceremonial magic. Similar to Gardnerian, but covens work robed.

Creabh Ruadh Tradition   The Irish "Red Branch" male mysteries tradition.

Cymri Tradition   Pre-Celtic path, main pagan traditions of Wales.

Druidiactos   Cultural, magical, and religious Druidic path.

Druidic Traditions   Magical traditions based on Druidic philosophy, rituals, and practices.

Dryad Tradition   Feminist Druidic path that incorporates Faery tradition.

Eclectic Celtic Wicca   Many practicing Wiccans, both solitary and groups, call themselves eclectic because they combine the elements of other mystery traditions and the Celtic deities with other pantheons together into one.

Eireannach Tradition   The various Irish paths.

Faery Tradition   Based on the Tuatha De Danann, a living tradition made popular by R. J. Stewart.

Faery Wicca   Faery and Wicca blended together into one; one of the oldest folk traditions. Self-initiation is discouraged, but acceptable. Up until current times, this tradition was only taught orally by teacher to student.

Gaelic Tradition   The Irish and Scottish traditions.

Gardnerian Wicca   Denomination of the craft that published its secret knowledge in 1954; named for Gerald Gardner. A Wicca tradition that takes its *Book of Shadows* from Doreen Valiente and other various sources. Covens work skyclad with an emphasis on the Goddess. Consists of a degree system of advancement, and self-initiation is discouraged.

Gwyddonic Druid Tradition   Welsh initiatory Druid tradition, based on the Concept of Oneness with some Wicca blended in. Led by a high priestess and high priest, solitary practitioners or groups work robed, with a degree system of advancement. Up until 1994, this tradition was taught orally by teacher to student(s) in secret Druidic Colleges.

Hebridean Tradition   Scottish tradition based on the Irish myths.

Hibernian Tradition   An Irish tradition from the Middle Ages, with Roman influence.

Irish Tradition   Many individual Irish traditions native to Ireland (some pre-Celtic).

Kingstone Tradition   An English tradition that has Celtic roots.

Maidenhill Tradition   Mother Goddess and Horned God tradition founded in England in 1970s.

Majestic Tradition   An English tradition that sees monarchs as sacrificial kings and fertility queens.

Manx Tradition   An Irish tradition with roots on the Isle of Man. Manannan Mac Llyr is a principle deity.

North Country Tradition   The pagan tradition of the Yorkshire area of England.

North Isles Tradition   Norse-influenced tradition of Orkney and the Shetland Islands.

Northern Tradition   Celtic and Norse blending of paths, sometimes called Asatru.

The Order of Bards, Ovates, and Druids   Popular Celtic experienced-based Druidism.

Pecti-Wita   Scottish solitary path of the Picts, a pre-Celtic people of northern Scotland. A tradition passed on by Aidan Breac, which is attuned to lunar and solar changes.

Reformed Druids   Tradition organized in Minnesota in 1963.

Romano-Gaulish Tradition   Combination of Celtic and Roman Pagan practices.

Sacred Wheel Tradition   Neo-pagan Wiccan path with Celtic overtones.

Scotia Tradition   Path that includes old Iberian (Spanish) pagan practices and beliefs.

Scottish Tradition   Catch-term for traditions native to Scotland (some pre-Celtic).

Seax-Wicca   Founded by Raymond Buckland in 1973, Wicca with a Saxon basis. Democratic organization with either coven or solitary practitioners.

Shamanic Traditions   An ancient pre-Celtic tradition focusing on shape-shifting, spirit helpers, shamanic journeying, and ancestral contact.

Tuatha De Danann   Irish path based on the legends and myths of the Tuatha De Danann, the Celtic Gods and Goddesses.

Ueleda Tradition   Initiatory Druidic tradition of all women.

Welsh Traditions   The name for the many pagan traditions stemming from Wales.

West Country Tradition   Pagan tradition of southwestern England, particularly Devonshire and Cornwall.

Wicca   The craft of the wise, usually referring to an Anglo-Celtic practice; nonexclusive spiritual path, often integrating many different pantheons such as Celtic, Greek, Roman, and Egyptian.

Witan Tradition   Celtic, Scottish, Pictish, and Norse traditions blended together into one Scottish tradition (self-initiatory); Goddess oriented nature-based, fertility religion.

Witchcraft   Practicing the art and craft; often refers to those of Celtic and Anglo traditions, but actually much broader based, including several pagan paths. The Druidesses were called witches by the Christians.

Wittan Tradition   Old Irish traditions combined with Norse influences. Self-initiation and solitary practice accepted.

Y Tylwyth Teg Tradition   Founded in the United States by Bill Wheeler in 1967, a Welsh-based path that combines Irish myth, legend, folk, and Faery lore.

Types of Celtic Groups

Circle   Often an informal and loosely knit group of people who gather together to do ritual and/or magic. Sometimes there is a hierarchy, in the sense that there are group leaders or orchestrators. Once in a while members of other groups join together with a circle for ritual or celebration, particularly public ritual.

Clan (Not to be confused with traditional Scottish clans)   A large, informal pagan group, with both an inner and outer court. The majority of members are in the outer court, with the inner court reserved for covens, groves, colleges, and circles who belong to the clan. Sharing knowledge within the clan is a priority, as are the celebration of the eight Celtic festivals.

Coven   A small, tightly knit, closed group of people, generally numbering from three to thirteen, led by a priestess and generally a priest as well, but not necessarily. Proportionately female and male is best for balance in the coven. An initiatory process and degrees are common in covens, with personal teachings provided by the priestess and priest. Ideally, in a coven there needs to be a great deal of trust, love, and cooperation, which is sometimes difficult to achieve when you get a group of people together (any group of people).

Druidic College   A small or large group, up to fifty members, with by-laws, that comes together for rituals, feasting, and metaphysical discussions on the eight festival days and full Moons. Led by an elected high priestess and high priest, with the priestess's word being the final one. In has three degrees or badges of instruction (first, second, third), usually one-on-one, with the student being responsible for asking his or her teacher metaphysical questions. The aim is to complete training as Bard, Vates, and Druid, becoming a thrice master or craft master.

Grove   An organized pagan group of people who come together for festivals and worship. The focus in groves is on the teachings and experienced-based ritual, utilizing the three gates and three worlds. Groves are fast becoming more popular in America because outsiders are welcome to their open circle and they perform their rituals outdoors, preferably in the woods.

Solitary (hedge)   A practitioner who practices magic and does ritual alone. Sometimes solitary practitioners get together for rituals once or twice a year with other practitioners or groups. This group is the largest growing body of pagans today.

Tribe   Several clans make up a tribe, often from the same general geographical area. Sometimes tribes descend from a common ancestor from mythology, or from a particular clan or coven. Tribes are independent communities, with class stratification. The tribal leader is the king, queen, or chieftain. The spiritual leader of the tribe is the Druis. Rules, laws, and regulations often apply to tribes. The tribe gathers once a year, and sometimes more often on special festivals.

Celtic Wicca

Wicca is the modern revival and renewal of a nature-oriented, Earth-spirited practice derived from the pre-Christian religion called the Old Religion or Goddess Religion, often referred to as the Mystery Traditions. The actual origins of contemporary Wicca owe much to Charles Leland (Aradia), Gerald Gardner, Aleister Crowley, Doreen Valiente, and Alex Sanders, among others. Now, Wicca has evolved away from the "old school" attitudes of its founders to a "new school" feel, which is more open-ended and eclectic, with less structure and more do's than don'ts.

Difficult to define, Celtic Wicca covers at least eight countries, combining the mythological traditions from those areas, especially Ireland, Wales, Scotland, England, and Brittany. Primarily, Celtic Wicca centers around Welsh and English mystery traditions, particularly Druidism and Faery, and also on natural "elemental" magic.

The American forms of Celtic Wicca are extremely tolerant of different points of view and lifestyles, but all are dedicated to the responsible stewardship and protection of the Earth and to the positive evolution of consciousness. Celtic Wicca is a popular and appealing tradition whose main focus is to re-link humanity with itself and nature.

The religious practice of witchcraft provides a formula for

spiritual development. Celtic Wicca is all about self-discovery, change, and personal empowerment. Wicca is a participatory revelation and a celebratory action leading to a more expanded understanding of oneself and the universe. Through myth, ritual, poetry, music, lovemaking, and working in harmony with the Mother, the sacred Earth, practitioners awaken the divine within and the magic of every moment. It's all about the pre-Christian Goddesses and Gods, about spirit and ancestral power, and not about Satan or the devil, which are Christian constructs.

Modern Celtic traditions, in particular Wicca, focus on working for the good of the sacred Earth, encouraging the development of positive, practical, intuitive, and artistic abilities, including but not limited to:

Acting, alternative healing, alternate lifestyles, animal husbandry, astrology and astronomy, brewing and wine making, camping, canning and drying foods, computer and Internet skills, cooking, craftwork, crocheting, dancing, dowsing and other divination practices, drawing, electronics, embroidery, entrepreneurial skills, environmental concerns and preservation, filmmaking, gardening and agriculture, herbal craft, lovemaking, lucid dreaming skills, metalwork, music, painting, parenting skills, poetry, pottery and sculpture, publishing, quilting, recording, retailing, sailing, sewing, solar, water, and wind power, song, theater production, weaving, writing, and woodworking.

Celtic Wiccans follow the Wheel of the Year, marking the paths of the Sun and Moon by celebrating eight solar festivals and thirteen lunar festivals. In addition, many Wiccans use the different phases of the Moon to do particular types of ritual, magic, and spellworking. For example, personal protection spells are best done during the dark of the Moon.

Ceremonial magic is part of Celtic Wicca, taking the form of high magic, and was developed by Eliphas Levi, Dion Fortune,

S. L. MacGregor Mathers, Dr. W. Wynn Westcott, A. E. Waite, the previously mentioned Aleister Crowley, Paul Foster Case, and Israel Regardie, among others. Many of these people went on to form their own branches of mystery traditions.

Due to its inclusive, rather than exclusive, nature, many women have embraced Celtic Wicca as a path of empowerment after thousands of years of patriarchal oppression. Another reason women like Celtic Wicca and paganism is because there exists a disheartening lack of women in positions of power in the major religions throughout the world. The high priestess or designated woman, representing the Goddess in Wiccan ritual, is often the leader and has final say in all matters. In all Celtic Wiccan traditions I have participated in, the priestess or woman is definitely equal to, if not more powerful, than the high priest or man.

Besides attracting women, modern Celtic Wicca also appeals to men, as it allows men to better understand both their masculine and feminine sides through powerful ritual, music, spell-working, and divine rapport. One of the more obvious benefits for women and men with interests in Celtic traditions is that joining a coven, college, grove, or other group is a great way to meet like-minded, potential partners, whatever your sexual preference. As you read this book, hundreds if not thousands of people are meeting other pagans on the Internet. The challenge in the years ahead will be to continue to create an atmosphere of mutual support, connection, cohesive organization, and interest among pagans of all traditions in a seemingly chaotic and disconnected world.

The fact that there are no set rules and regulations in Celtic Wicca also holds great appeal for other independent thinkers such as lesbians, gays, crossdressers, and those who have had or are contemplating sex change operations, as well as lower-, middle-, and upper-class families, homemakers, doctors, psychologists, lawyers, teachers, teens, and children. Kids are particularly interested in nature and animals, so Celtic traditions and paganism are natural paths for them. Teens respond to the independent, innovative, and romantic nature of Celtic spirituality. As Celtic Wicca becomes more accepted by society, more and more people are coming out of the proverbial "broom closet."

Some Celtic Wiccans are solitary practitioners, while others participate in groups. Most practitioners do a bit of both. Regardless whether you practice solo or with others, contemporary Celtic Wiccan ceremonies often include music, poetry, dance, ritual and healing works, as well as toasting the Goddesses, Gods, and ancestors, visualization, having fun, metaphysical discussion, and feasting. Most Celtic groups wear craft robes or traditional garb such as kilts for their ceremonies, but some go nude (or skyclad).

The Philosophy of Celtic Wicca

Celtic Wicca is an Earth religion or spirituality, which is the primary reason I was personally drawn to the tradition. Like all pagans, Celtic Wiccans revere nature as the foremost teacher. By observing her cycles and movements, it is possible to attune to her rhythms, tapping in and pooling her knowledge for use in daily life. In doing so, you also align yourself with the Goddesses, Gods, and other light beings, crossing the Otherworldly threshold for a few moments now and again and penetrating the veils of the many dimensions of experience and spirit.

Nature mirrors Oneness, deity, and creative power and as such is considered the blueprint of spirit. Practitioners of Celtic traditions and Wicca, like many of those who study the Western mysteries, embrace the concept that everything mirrors everything else: as above, so below. Cloning has given new meaning to this concept, where a duplicate organism, including a human being, can be created or reborn from a single cell.

Carrying this a step further, Wiccans feel that creation mirrors the nature of the Creatrix/Creator, just as a song mirrors the qualities and experiences of the songwriter. Gaining rapport with nature—for example, through shape-shifting techniques— helps to heighten your awareness and expand your perception, enabling you to tap into the pure creative energies or spirit of Oneness.

Divine presence and communion are mainstays of all Celtic traditions. Divine guidance is a blessing and a boon. It is from deity that we derive sustenance. Wiccans honor nature in the forms of the Triple Goddess and the Horned God. Deities have solar, stellar, lunar, and Earthly aspects and embody the Upper World, Middle World, and Underworld.

Considered to be pure creative and inspirational power, spiritual energies and deities stem from Oneness and are manifested through the feminine and masculine polarities represented by the Goddess and God. Most Celtic Wiccans feel that a balance, integration, and understanding of the feminine and masculine polarities are essential for well-being and for the evolution of consciousness. The divine joining of these polarities takes place in sacred sex, and Wiccans consider sexuality to be especially sacred and one of the most powerful, if not *the* most powerful, sources of magical and spiritual energy.

Rebirth is a basic teaching in Celtic Wicca and most magical traditions. Wiccans, particularly hereditary witches, take stock of genetic memory, knowing, as Raven Gramasi writes in *Wiccan Mysteries,* "that each of us carries the 'essential distillation' of the memories of all of our ancestors within our DNA. . . . In a metaphysical sense this provides us with a channel to the past through which we can awaken the memories of past pagan practices."

Reincarnation, with the soul passing through many lives and being reborn, is a cornerstone of Celtic Wiccan philosophy. References to reincarnation appear in "The Witches' Creed" ("immortal and ever-renewing"), and in "The Charge of the Goddess" ("beyond death I give peace, and freedom, and reunion with those who have gone before").

In Celtic Wicca, the afterlife is lived in the Otherworld, Tirnan-Og, the Land of Youth, also called Avalon, the Land of Apples. Spirit rests here, connects with those who have gone before and with deity, and is then reborn into the physical realm.

Some Wiccan mystery traditions adhere to the theory of seven dimensions: ultimate, divine, spiritual, mental, astral, elemental, and physical. In Norse mythology nine world levels exist. They are Asgard, Vanaheim, Lightalheim, which are the three higher or celestial levels. The next three worlds are Midgard (Earth), Muspelheim (the world of creative and destructive fire), and Nifelheim (the world of creative and destructive frost). The last three world levels are the subterranean worlds of Swartalfheim, Hel, and Jotunheim. The Druid tradition proposes four levels of the Otherworld: (1) Annwyn, the first level and closest to the mortal realm; (2) Gwynvyd, the second level; (3) Cengant, the monadic realm; and (4) the abyss, called Cynthral.

Frequently, the reason people become interested in Wicca is because they want to learn how to do magic. Celtic traditions such as Celtic Wicca and Druidism teach basic metaphysical principles, such as how to manifest your intentions into reality. Learning more about magic was a motivating factor for me to take up a Druid tradition, and it continues to amaze me as I discover more each day.

Another reason many people are becoming interested in Celtic traditions is because many of us have Celtic roots. Since visiting Scotland, Wales, and England when I was sixteen, my fascination with Celtic traditions and practices has continually increased.

Celtic traditions give us an opportunity to connect with our roots and with the very spirit of the sacred land, the Earth. Inclusive rather than exclusive, Wicca does not require anyone to accept a common path or share belief systems, but instead focuses on tapping into nature's rhythms and cycles by merging with nature and following the paths of the Sun, Moon, and Stars. Rituals and spellworking are ways of keying into these cycles and natural patterns.

The Concept of Oneness

Everything is energy, and although different polarities exist, all energy is One. The energetic polarities used in magic are positive, negative, and neutral. Positive energy constructs patterns and spells while negative energy breaks up patterns of energy. Neutrality has the potential to become either positive or negative, or to remain neutral.

The Concept of Oneness is in alignment with many Celtic Wicca traditions. It is open-ended, simply stating that all things are One, whatsoever they may be—everything. All things connect and weave into One Boundless Being, regardless of energy state, density, form, color, vibration, duration, and so forth. Every aspect of Oneness is unique, yet each aspect is fully the One, and Boundless—and more.

The Concept of Oneness forms the essential DNA of all magic. Your magical ability becomes directly proportional to your comprehension and understanding of this simple concept. Oneness is a state of mind, a crossroads where all energies connect. As you turn your mind more often toward Oneness in your everyday life, you will find that this concept changes from an intellectual idea into actual experience. The key is to be patient and to keep consistently and continuously turning your mind to Oneness.

One exercise I have found particularly helpful for accessing Oneness is by becoming everything in my immediate environment, from the lamp to the paperclip, from the computer disk to the spider web in the corner. When you are alone, for example, say aloud, "I am the lamp, the lamp is me, we are one. I am the spider web, the spider web is me, we are one." Do this with everything you are aware of in one room of your house, or while walking in the woods, or at the ocean. This will hone your ability to merge and become One with all things.

Celtic Wiccan Spiritual Practices

Celtic Wicca spiritual practices include, but are not limited to:

1. Divine rapport with Goddesses and Gods
2. Ritual and magical practice and knowledge
3. Using spells, symbols, charms, potions, and enchantments
4. Dreaming practices such as lucid dreaming and doubling out
5. Development of psychic and intuitive abilities and skills
6. Fasting for mental clarity and visions
7. Physical disciplines for strengthening body, mind, and spirit
8. Drawing, raising, and directing personal power and energy
9. Visualization, meditation, and guided imagery
10. Controlled use of psychoactive drugs
11. Astral projection, out-of-body travel, and psycho-navigation
12. Shape-shifting and transmigration
13. Sex magic

Wiccan Ethics

Basically a nonviolent and exceptionally tolerant philosophy, Wicca is an inclusive tradition rather than an exclusive one. Accepting of most beliefs and lifestyles, Wiccans have a great respect for the sacred Earth, the Goddess, God, and for all life, human and otherwise.

All things are One, whatsoever they may be, and thus everything in the cosmos is connected and related. Every action, thought, dream, sensation, and so forth affects everything else. We are woven into one infinite web, and Wiccan focuses on working with the infallible laws of nature rather than with the less than perfect human laws. We are willing to accept responsibility for our actions and the outcome, preferring to live each day with our eyes wide open rather than exist in a state of permanent somnambulance.

Wiccans follow the "Wiccan Rede" and "The Three-Fold Law" as formulas for ethical and moral behavior within the traditions. No special rules of conduct apply, as Wicca is generally devoid of dogma. The steadfast rule is to manipulate and direct energies toward a particular purpose but not to manipulate people.

The Wiccan Rede states that a positive and beneficial intention is paramount in all magical work. There are ways of doing protection spells for you and those you love without inflicting physical, mental, or spiritual (psychic) harm. Most spells are directed toward a specific end, formulated only after much thought, and they customarily end with the phrase "for the good of all and the harm of none." Wiccans learn how to deflect harm without causing harm by neutralizing negative energies and casting them back into the cosmos to be neutralized or diminished.

The last "Rede" line, "An ye harm none, do what ye will," means to find your purpose in life and to fulfill it, in a way that will benefit you and not harm others. By finding your purpose, you discover the divine nature within, experiencing the freedom to do what you feel most strongly about in your head and heart without harming others.

The Three-Fold Law of Return popularized by Gerald Gardner reinforces the idea of focusing on positive acts rather than negative ones. It says that if you do good, then you will receive good three times over. On the other hand, if you do harm, you will receive the same three times over. In other words, both positive and negative energy return back to their originator, often stronger than they were directed outward. There is also the seven-fold, nine-fold, and hundred-fold return law, especially in spellwork.

The Law of Return, whatever its number or power, basically means, if you send out good vibes and do positive magic, that's what you get in return. If you do negative works of magic or attack others, then that is what you will receive in return. For the most part, the Three-Fold Law of Return keeps practitioners honest and truthful, and their intentions good.

Those of us who follow Wicca are independent thinkers, who actively and intelligently defend ourselves when attacked by others. We do not accept abuse or mistreatment from others, and do not ignore darkness and evil, hoping it will go away. Instead, we act upon our spiritual center, cultivating positive patterns and eliminating negative ones by responding to the messages from the Goddesses, Gods, our ancestors, and from the sacred Earth.

Wiccan Spiritual Texts

These powerful spiritual texts are used by many Celtic Wiccans in ritual and magical work. By reading them over carefully, you will find, for the most part, that they are self-explanatory.

The texts give a set of instructions to gain rapport with the spirit of the Goddess, God, and Oneness. They are to be read out loud in ritual, inside the circle, grove, or sacred space. For example, "The Wiccan Rede," "Charge of the God," and "Charge of the Goddess" can be read out loud during wiccaning, handfasting, and initiation ceremonies, as well as during sabbat circles any time you desire to bring the divine presence of the God and Goddess into the circle and to build divine energy. The "Charge of the Goddess" is traditionally read during the "Drawing Down the Moon" ritual. The "Invocation of the Horned God" can be read out loud at sabbat rituals. "Drawing

Down the Moon" is used to invoke the Great Goddess during
Full Moon celebrations.

THE WICCAN REDE
(Modern Version)

Bide ye Wiccan laws you must,
in perfect love and perfect trust.
Live ye must and let to live,
fairly take and fairly give.

For the circle thrice about
to keep unwelcome spirits out.
To bind ye spell well every time,
let the spell be spake in rhyme.

Soft of eye and light of touch,
speak ye little, listen much.
Deosil go by the waxing moon,
chanting out ye baleful tune.

When ye Lady's moon is new,
kiss ye hand to her times two.
When ye moon rides at her peak,
then ye heart's desire seek.

Heed the North wind's mighty gale,
lock the door and trim the sail.
When the wind comes from the South,
Love will kiss thee on the mouth.

When the wind blows from the East,
expect the new and set the feast.
Nine woods in the cauldron go,
burn them fast and burn them slow.

Elder be ye Lady's tree,
burn it not, or cursed ye'll be.
When the wheel begins to turn,
soon ye Beltane fires will burn.

When the wheel hath turned a Yule,
light the log the Horned One rules.
Heed ye flower, bush, and tree,
by the Lady blessed be.

Where the rippling waters go,
cast a stone, the truth ye'll know.
When ye have and hold a need,
harken not to other's greed.

With a fool no season spend,
or be counted as his friend.
Merry meet and merry part,
bright the cheeks and warm the heart.

Mind ye threefold law ye should,
three times bad and three times good.
When misfortune is enow,
wear the star upon thy brow.

True in love may ye ever be,
lest thy love be false to thee.
These eight words the Wiccan Rede fulfill;
An harm ye none, do what ye will.

THE WITCHES' CREED—THE REDE OF THE WICCAE
(by Doreen Valiente, from *Witchcraft for Tomorrow*)

Hear now the word of the Witches,
the secrets we hid in the night,

When dark was our destiny's pathway,
That now we bring forth in the light.

Mysterious Water and Fire,
The Earth and the wide-ranging Air,
By hidden Quintessence we know Them,
and we will keep silent and dare.

The birth and rebirth of all Nature,
the passing of Winter and Spring,
We share with the life Universal,
Rejoice in the Magical Ring.

Four times in the year the Great Sabbat,
Returns, and the Witches are seen,
At Lammas and Candlemas dancing,
on May Eve and old Hallowe'en.

When day-time and night-time are equal,
When sun is at greatest and least,
The four Lesser Sabbats are summoned,
Again Witches gather in feast.

Thirteen silver moons in a year are,
Thirteen is the Coven's array,
Thirteen times at Esbat make merry,
For each golden year and a day.

The power was passed down the ages,
Each time between woman and man
Each century unto the other,
Ere time and the ages began.

When drawn is the Magical circle,
By sword or athame or power,
Its compass between two worlds lies,
In the Land of Shades for that hour.

This world has no right then to know it,
And the world beyond will tell naught,
The oldest of Gods are invoked there,
The Great Work of magic is wrought.

For two are the mystical pillars,
That stand at the gate of the shrine,
And two are the powers of Nature,
The forms and the forces divine.

The Dark and the Light in succession,
The opposites each unto each,
Shown forth as a God and a Goddess:
Of this did our ancestors teach.

By night he's the wild wind's rider,
The Horn'd One, the Lord of the Shades.
By day he's the King of the Woodland,
The dweller in green forest glades.

She is youthful or old as she pleases,
She sails the torn clouds in her barque,
The bright Silver Lady of Midnight,
The Crone who weaves spells in the dark.

The Master and Mistress of magic,
They dwell in the deep of the Mind,
Immortal and ever-renewing,
With power to Free or to Bind.

So drink the wine to the Old Gods,
And Dance and Make Love in their praise,
Till Elphame's Fair Land shall receive us
In Peace at the end of our days.

And Do What You Will be the challenge,
So be it in Love that harms none,
For this is the only commandment,
By Magic of old, be it done!

Eight words the Witches' Creed fulfill:
If it harms none, Do what you will!

CHARGE OF THE GODDESS
(by Gerald Gardner, from Stewart Farrar,
What Witches Do)

Whenever you have need of anything, once in the month and better when the moon is full, then shall you assemble in some secret place and adore the spirit of me, who am Queen of all witches. There shall ye assemble, ye who are fain to learn all sorcery, yet have not won its deepest secrets; to these will I teach all things that are as yet unknown. And ye shall be free from slavery; and as a sign that ye be truly free, you shall be naked in your rites; and ye shall dance, sing, feast, make music and love, all in my praise. For mine is the ecstasy of the spirit, and mine also is joy on earth; for my law is love unto all beings. Keep pure your highest ideals; strive ever towards them, let nothing stop you or turn you aside. For mine is the secret door which opens upon the Land of Youth, and mine is the cup of the wine of life, and the Cauldron of Cerridwen, which is the Holy Vessel of Immortality. I am the gracious Goddess, who gives the gift of joy unto the heart of man. Upon earth, I give the knowledge of the spirit eternal; and beyond death, I give peace, and freedom, and reunion with those who have gone before. Nor do I demand sacrifice; for behold, I am the Mother of all living, and my love is poured out upon the earth.

I am the beauty of the green earth, and the white moon among the stars, and the mystery of the waters, and the desire of the heart of man. Call unto thy soul, arise, and come unto me. For I am the soul of Nature, who gives life to the Universe. From me all things proceed, and unto me all things must return; and before my face, beloved of Gods and of men, let thine innermost divine self be enfolded in the rapture of the infinite. Let my worship be within the heart that rejoicest; for behold, all acts of love and pleasure are my rituals. Therefore, let there be beauty and strength, power and compassion, honor and humility, mirth and reverence within you. And thou who thinketh to seek for me, know thy seeking and yearning shall avail thee not unless thou knoweth the mystery; that if that which thy seekest thou findest not within thee, thou wilt never find it without thee. For behold, I have been with thee from the beginning; and I am that which is attained at the end of desire.

CHARGE OF THE GOD
(by Gerald Gardner, from Stewart Farrar's book,
What Witches Do)

Listen to the words of the Great Father, who of old was called Osiris, Adonis, Zeus, Thor, Pan, Cernunnos, Herne, Lugh, and by many other names. My law is harmony with all things. Mine is the secret that opens the gates of life and mine is the dish of salt of the earth that is the body of Cernunnos that is the eternal circle of rebirth. I give the knowledge of life everlasting, and beyond death I give the promise of regeneration and renewal. I am the sacrifice, the father of all things, and my protection blankets the earth.

Hear the words of the dancing God, the music of whose laughter stirs the winds, whose voice calls the seasons. I who am the Lord of the Hunt and the Power of the Light, sun among the clouds and the secret of the flame. I call upon your bodies to arise and come unto me. For I am the flesh of the earth and all its beings. Through me all things must die and with me are reborn. Let my worship be in the body that sings, for behold all acts of willing sacrifice are my rituals. Let there be desire and fear, anger and weakness, joy and peace, awe and longing within you. For these, too, are part of the mysteries found within yourself, within me, all beginnings have endings, and all endings have beginnings.

DRAWING DOWN THE MOON
(from *The Grimoire of Lady Sheba*)

All ye assembled at mine shine,
Mother Darksome and Divine.
Mine the Scourge and mine the Kiss,
Here I charge you in this sign
All ye assembled in my sight,
Bow before my spirit bright,
Aphrodite, Arianrod,
Lover of the Horned God.
Mighty Queen of Witchery and night,
Morgan, Etoine, Nisene,
Diana, Bridgid, Melusine,
Am I named of old by men,
Artemis and Cerridwen,
Hell's dark mistress, Heaven's Queen.
Ye who ask of me a rune
Or would ask of me a boon,
meet me in some secret glade,
Dance my round in greenwood shade,
by the light of the Full Moon.
In a place, wild and lone,
dance about mine altar stone;
work my holy mystery.
Ye who are feign to sorcery,
I bring ye secrets yet unknown.

No more shall ye know slavery,
who gave true worship unto me.
Ye who tred my round on Sabbat night,
come ye naked to the rite,
in token ye be really free,
I teach ye the mystery of rebirth,
work ye my mysteries in mirth.
Heart joined to heart and lip to lip,
five are the points of fellowship,
that bring ye ecstasy on Earth,
for I am the circle of rebirth.
I ask no sacrifice, but do bow,
no other Law but Love I know,
by naught but love may I be known.
All things living are mine own,
from me they come, to me they go.

I invoke Thee and call upon Thee
Mighty Mother of us all.
Bringer of Fruitfulness by seed and by root.
I invoke Thee by stem and by bud.
I invoke Thee by life and love
and call upon thee to descend into the body
of this Thy Priestess and Servant,
Hear with her ears, speak with her tongue,
touch with her hands, kiss with her lips,
that Thy servants may be fulfilled.

INVOCATION OF THE HORNED GOD
(from *The Grimoire of Lady Sheba*)

By the flame that burneth bright,
O' Horned One!

We call thy name into the night,
O' Ancient One!

Thee we invoke, by the moon-led sea,
By the standing stone and the twisted tree.
Thee we invoke where gather thine own,
By the nameless shrine forgotten and lone.

Come where the round of the dance is trod,
Horn and hoof of the goatfoot God!
By moonlit meadow, on dusky hill,
When the haunted wood is hushed and still.

Come to the charm of the chanted prayer,
As the moon bewitches the midnight air.
Evoke thy powers, that potent bide
In shining stream and the secret tide.

In fiery flame by starlight pale,
In shadowy host that rides the gale,
And by the fern-brakes fairy-haunted
Of forests wild and woods enchanted.

Come! Come!
To the heart-beats drum!
Come to us who gather below
When the broad white moon is climbing slow

Through the stars to the heaven's height
We hear thy hoofs on the wind of night!
As black tree-branches shake and sigh,
By joy and terror we know thee nigh.

We speak the spell thy power unlocks
At Solstice, Sabbat, and equinox

The Elements

The elements of earth (north), air (east), fire (south), and water (west or in all directions), with the fifth element being spirit (center) are customary in Celtic Wiccan traditions. These key elements are integrated in both rituals and magical works. Each element is represented on the altar by your magical tools.

Enhance your connection with the elements by associating them with areas of your being. Verbally remind yourself that you are the elements. Chant these words:

> My flesh and bones are the earth. The earth is my flesh and bones. We are one. My breath is the air. The air is my breath. We are one. My eyes are the light. The light is my eyes. We are one. My emotions are water. Water is my emotions. We are one.

The more you practice this, the closer your rapport with the elements.

Some practitioners feel the element should be able to destroy the tool which corresponds to it. I feel that the element should be able to create the tool associated with it.

Magical Tools

Visual and kinesthetic, tools are used for triggering whole-brain activity, balancing both right and left brain activity. Your magical tools are imbued with the sacred energies of the Goddess and God and are energetically alive. While it is true that you need no special tools for working magic, implements that you gather together, consecrate, and use regularly in ritual and magic become more than just symbols that trigger your subconscious; they become essentially alive and a part of you. That is why it is important to be extra careful when giving away to others any magical tools you have used for a number of years. I have found that even when you clear them out through traditional and magical methods, a residue of your energy or morphogenic field remains within the actual atomic structure of the tool. They are, in essence, imprinted with your energy signature.

In the Celtic Druid tradition, there are six tools of the art and craft gathered together and used to make powerful and potent magic. Each of these six tools and their contents represent each of the elements upon the altar as follows:

TOOL	ELEMENT
The Bowl	Earth
The Wand	Air
The Athame	Fire
The Chalice	Water
The Incense Holder	Air
The Candle Holder (white candle)	Fire

Optional altar items:
- Red or green altar cloth
- 2 Additional candle holders and sticks to be used on altar, 1 red and 1 green (representing God and Goddess)
- Additional altar cup or chalice for wine or juice

You will also need:
- A journal to record your ritual experiences
- A 9-foot-long cord
- A ritual robe or tunic

In Celtic Wicca, magical tools are used for ritual and also for spellwork. Several other kinds of tools besides the previously mentioned are used. Following is an alphabetical inventory of Wiccan magical tools:

Athame   Double-edged dagger or knife, best purchased new and unused by anyone else. Can be used in ritual and magic to cut the sacred circle and open spiritual doors, and is also used practically to cut food, to incise candles in candle magic, to carve runes on items, and for protection. The athame's edges are often dulled for safer ritual use. Generally, the symbol of the creative Fire, magical power, and the South point, a few traditions link the athame, Air element, and East Quadrant together. In Pecti-Wita (a Scottish solitary path), the dirk is the equivalent of the athame, but generally has a longer blade.

Bell   A feminine symbol of the Goddess, the bell is used in ritual by some Wiccan traditions. The bell is rung one, two, or three times throughout a ritual to create the optimum vibration or frequency. In the Druid tradition I was trained in, we do not use bells, but in practice I have found tingsha bells to be particularly useful in clearing out negative energies and calling in deities.

Besom   A broom made of straw or grass or a leafy branch of pine, oak, fir, lavender, rosemary, and so forth, used to clean your ritual circle of all negative and unwanted energies. Start in the center of your circle and move clockwise (sunwise), sweeping from the center outward. While doing this, visualize the area being washed energetically with a cobalt blue light. I tied together a combination of herbs and branches gathered from the forest near my home for my besom and use it mainly for outdoor ritual work.

Bolline   Traditionally, a white-handled knife used for cutting herbs, carving symbols, cutting cords, and so forth. Used in place of the athame for physical or practical cutting, while the athame is often reserved for ritual work. (I do not use a bolline, but use my athame for both ritual and practical cutting.)

Book of Shadows   Traditionally, a private, personal journal of your magical experiences. Often rituals, spells, thoughts, ideas, and divine communications are written in this book.

Candles   Associated with the Fire and Air elements; almost always used on the altar for ritual and magic. Specific colors are used for specific purposes. On the Druid's altar, a green candle is used for the Goddess and a red candle is used for the God, with the white candle representing spirit.

Cauldron   Often used in Celtic traditions, the cauldron is three-legged with its opening smaller than its base, that is very womb-like. The cauldron represents the Goddess and the Water element and is usually made of black cast iron. Candles can be set inside the cauldron and allowed to safely burn out. The cauldron can also be used for scrying when filled with water or oil.

Chalice or Cup   Symbol of Water and the West, the chalice or cup holds water or wine. It is a vessel made of metal, stone, clay, or glass, often representing the "loving or divine" cup of the Goddess. Some traditions feel that Water is the element representing all directions, not just the Western quadrant. Only use lead-free pewter chalices or cups.

Cord   Symbolic of the cord of life, it measures nine feet long with a knot at one end to anchor it to a stick, and knots at 4½ feet, 6½ feet, and 7½ feet. It can be used to draw a pentacle or a magical circle or simply to wrap around the waist of your robe. The rolled measuring cord and rod were used by the astronomer-priest(ess) to assure the precise astronomical orientation of temples in ancient times. Some traditions use certain colors of cords to designate degrees.

Crystals and Gemstones   Each crystal and gemstone has unique qualities that can be utilized in ritual and magic. They are gifts of the Earth and natural amplifiers of thoughtforms and divine energies. Stones make excellent communication tools, watchtower or ward markers, altar tools, and tips on wands, as well as healing tools, divination devices, and circle markers.

Drum   A bridge to the spirit or Otherworld. A magical tool of vibration and sound, associated with the Air and Earth elements. Excellent for enhancing focus and merging. The head of a person's drum is sometimes broken when he or she dies as a way to free the person's spirit.

Fetish   Often carved of stone or wood, or made of clay, fetishes can be in the shape of animals or more abstract symbols of the Goddess, God, ancestors, or the sacred spirits of the Earth; usually used as a powerful focus when doing a specific magical work. Fetishes can be made into ritual jewelry such as an amulet.

Incense Burner or Censor with Incense Representing the Fire and Air elements in ritual, the incense and incense burner are almost always used by all Celtic traditions in ritual and magic. A burner large enough to burn small papers is best. You can use a layer of sand or pebbles inside the burner as a base for the charcoal block(s). Potpads, handles, or a chain are advisable if you are going to move the burner while it is hot.

Oils and Herbs Associated with the many deities and all of the elements, both herbs and essential oils are used in ritual and magic. They are valued for their unique qualities and energies. Oils are used in incense and for anointing candles, magical tools, the altar, poppets, and the body. Herbs are burned over charcoal blocks as incense. They are used in candle magic and sachets, for offerings to the Goddess and God, as well as in ritual baths, cooking, and in herbal oils.

Pentacle Borrowed from ceremonial magic, the pentacle is the five-pointed star associated with the Earth element, used for protection and to evoke divine energies. Large and small pentacle shapes, sometimes natural such as sand dollars, or handmade, painted, or carved flat disks of wood and metal, and glass, are placed on the altar. Altar tile pentacles are popular today and are excellent ways of protecting your altar surface from melting wax and hot objects such as the lit incense burner. Pentacles are frequently worn as jewelry and sometimes hung over doors. The pentacle today is what the peace sign was in the sixties, a symbol of what some say is the fastest growing religion in America: Wicca.

Robe Your magical skin, made of any fabric, any color, any design. Your robe is reserved for ritual and magic. When you put your robe on, you automatically move into a magical frame of mind. Men sometimes wear kilts instead of robes. Contemporary groups often dispense with robes, wearing street clothes. Certain covens wear nothing at all, going skyclad.

Staff This Druidic tool sometimes represents authority and is used by many of those in Celtic traditions. Generally, at least shoulder high and about a half-inch in diameter, the staff holds and focuses magical energy, depending upon the wood it is made of, and is associated with the Earth element. (See Ogham Trees in chapter 4 for a complete listing.) A symbol of knowledge and very personal, staffs can be roughly hewn from a tree branch or carved with intricate patterns such as Celtic Knotwork, dragons, leaf and flower motifs, as well as runes, the Theban, and the Ogham. Best cut during a waxing moon and allowed to cure for an entire Moon cycle. Sometimes viewed as a combination of the sword and wand.

Sword   A tool of command and symbol of fire and the South, used to focus your will, magical power, and determination. Excellent tool for accessing ancestor energy and for magical protection. When choosing a sword, make certain it is easy to handle and use.

Talisman   Symbol of the Earth and the Northern quadrant, generally made of metal or stone, especially crystal and semi-precious stones. An object that is magically altered to contain and radiate a specific field and tone of energy. Often carried on your person and/or placed on your altar during ritual and spell-work to heighten the energies you are working with.

Wand   Associated with the East and the Air element and made from wood, metal, and/or stone, wands are shorter than staffs, usually no longer than the length of your forearm. Considered the most ancient of tools, the wand is used in ritual and magic to direct energies in specific patterns. Often used to bridge dimensions, to receive and send energetic patterns from here to there in such a way as to create a successful outcome in magical workings. Best cut during the waxing Moon and allowed to cure for an entire Moon cycle. (Note that some traditions associate the wand with fire and the South.)

Consecrating Your Magical Tools

Consecrate your tools and other altar objects by merging deeply with the divine energies of the Goddess and God, with the intention of imbuing the tools with the elemental qualities they embody. Make your items magical by merging and becoming one with the Goddess or God, and asking them to impart their divine energy and aspects into the object you are focusing upon. Visualize and sense the power of the Goddess and God, and then use your breath to physically pulse the divine energy into the item, by breathing in and sharply exhaling through your nose. Do this at least three times, and for better results, nine times. Your breath and focused intention are the carrier waves that move the energy into the tool.

If you wash your altar tools with dew before sunrise on May Day (Beltane) morning, it fills them with divine creative power and knowledge. As well as using dew to consecrate your tools, you can also use the four elements—Earth, Air, Fire, and Water—to charge your ritual tools and other items with powerful elemental energies.

Examine the energies of the tools you select and always clear the unwanted energies from them by smudging them with the smoke of sage and cedar. Some smudge sticks also have copal resin in them, which is excellent for this purpose. You can also pass your tools quickly and carefully through the flame of a sacred fire to cleanse them —for example, the flame of an altar candle. Or you can wash your tools in salt water or set them out in the sunlight or moonlight to clear them of negative energies. Also, herbs and oils are rubbed on tools to enhance their energies.

There are certain times of the day that are considered more energetically powerful: just before sunrise, sunrise, noon, sunset, twilight, moonrise, and midnight. Since ritual and magic are all about gathering and directing energies, you can make your ritual tools even more powerful by consecrating them at the appropriate (magical) time, which alters according to your intended use for the tool. For example, athames, swords, staffs, and wands are best consecrated at sunrise on a clear day, like Beltane morning. Use the power of the Sun's birth to fill yourself and then your tools with this energy. Other ideal times for consecrating altar tools such as your water chalice or cauldron are twilight, moonrise, and midnight on a Full Moon night.

In some Celtic traditions, it is customary for the high priestess and high priest to consecrate an initiate's tools directly after the initiation. In this case, the tools are placed under or to the left (Goddess side) of the altar during the initiation ceremony.

The Altar

Your altar is your magical working surface, considered the Lady's or Goddess' table. The altar holds the tools and elements and is a focal in ritual and magic (continue reading for examples of additional focals). It provides a sacred space at home. Just looking at an altar with its ritual tools, lit candles, and burning incense evokes a magical state of mind and the feeling of mystery.

Ideally, the altar is made of stone and hence serves to ground or eliminate any negative or unwanted energies. The best altar is a stone altar, symbolizing the Earth and the North point. Today many things are used for altars, from tables, desks, and chairs, to fireplace mantles, cardboard boxes, and the bare ground. Some practitioners leave their altars set up; other put their tools away after ritual and magical workings.

Some practitioners set their altar up in the North point because that is where you find yourself, on Earth. Others set the altar in the East point to correspond with the rising Sun. Still other practitioners place their altars in the center of their magical circle. Try several placements, and then select the one that feels right for you.

An altar cloth made of a natural material such as cotton, silk, velvet, or wool covers the altar. Soft pile fabrics such as velvet, velour, and ultrasuede are also popular choices. Generally red or green, it can be any color. Some practitioners embroider or paint runes, the Ogham, the Theban, or other magical symbols on their altar cloths. The right side of the altar is the power side, dedicated to the God. A red, gold, or orange candle and an appropriate God symbol—such as a statue or picture of a God, an obelisk, deer antlers, or other male representation—and the other masculine ritual tools such as your athame, incense burner, and sword are placed on the right-hand side. The left half of the altar is the nurturing side, dedicated to the Goddess. A green, white, or silver candle and an appropriate representation, plus the feminine ritual tools, such as the chalice of water, bowl of earth or salt, and the cauldron, are placed on the left side. If your cauldron is too large to put on the top of your altar, it can be placed on the floor to the left, or Goddess side, of the altar. The wine cup, a symbol of divine love, rests at the center of the altar. The besom is traditionally laid against the left side of the altar.

Keep your altar fluid, changing certain items such as flowers, stones, and so forth with the seasons as the Wheel of the Year turns. Be sure to place all of your tools and altar items so that you can use them at will. Each person using the altar customarily contributes something.

Prepare your sacred space by putting sea salt in a bowl of water. Taking a sprig of greenery, dip it into the salt water, and sprinkle your altar and ritual area in a clockwise (sunwise) motion as you say out loud in a clear voice (like you mean it!):

Begone from here all evil and foulness and darkness.
Begone from this place in Our Lady's Name!

Say this three times while visualizing a white light edged in cobalt blue clearing the area out energetically.

Before beginning ritual or magical work, set your altar table with everything you will need for your ritual and/or spellworking. Next, be sure to light the candles and incense. Traditionally, candles are allowed to burn out naturally. After you are done, pull up your circle and put everything away.

CDagical Focals

Focals, also called foci, are items used for focusing, amplifying, and concentrating magical energies. Choose your focals to blend well with the intention of your magical work or ritual. I strongly suggest that you use many focals together, such as candles, oils, stones, tools, foods, sound, and the like, which will engage your senses completely. The following is a list of magical focals:

Auditory Focals Music, sound, your voice, vibration, singing, chanting, drumming, humming, breathing, waterfalls, rivers, animal calls, the wind, falling rain or snow, oceans, fountains, and birds.

Gustatory Focals Food and beverages, the salt on your skin, things you can taste.

Intuitive Focals Items that represent a divine or magical experience you have had. Ritual jewelry, talismans, and certain symbols serve as intuitive focals, such as Oghams or runes from dream experiences.

Kinesthetic Focals The colors, textures, and shapes of things. Special textural fabrics such as velvet, carved chalices, and wands, all are excellent focals for touch.

Olfactory Focals Things you can smell, such as essential oils, foods, and incense.

Visual Focals Things you can see, such as photographs, symbols, drawings, paintings, statues; natural items, such as flowers, shells, crystals and gemstones, and the like.

The Three Eyes of Kerridwen

The natural progression of the mind is to move from intention and expectation, to desire, and then to merging—hence, the "Three Eyes of Kerridwen." Another perhaps simpler way to see the steps of "The Three Eyes" is to view them as: (A) conceiving, (B) creating, and (C) experiencing.

Basically a formula for patterning energy, "The Three Eyes of Kerridwen" provide a straightforward path that moves your mind energy from A to B to C. You can use this process in any magical work, including spellworking. First, you need to be very clear about your intention and what it is you expect, and, most of all, that you really want it. Second, you need to build a strong desire toward your intended creation. Third, you merge with Oneness as deeply as possible, and then a little deeper still, allowing your intention, expectation, and desire to flow out of you and circulate into Oneness. See and sense yourself releasing thought energy so powerful that this energy becomes manifested and created. All magical traditions involve gathering, moving, directing, and shaping energy into patterns, with merging as the key for facilitating the magic.

Merging

Merging is the natural feeling you get when you are in love or when you look into the eyes of your newborn baby. Merging is the sensation you get when watching the Sun set slowly across the valley, by walking in an old growth redwood forest, or sitting at the top of a mountain. Merging is the feeling that comes over you when you are in synchronicity with everything and at one with it all.

Merging connects you with Oneness and is the key to magical patterns and spellwork. You experience an awareness of Oneness when merging. Through this experience you begin to understand that Oneness is the true state of existence.

When you set out upon the Great Adventure, you primarily merge with the manifested universe, essentially comprised of existent energies. As your skills in the art and craft evolve and your awareness expands, you begin to merge with the unmanifested universe, the place where spontaneous creation circumvents "natural law." In this way, merging with Oneness becomes your gateway to other thresholds and dimensions of experience.

Within this context, merging also provides a way for moving beyond the parameters of time and space. By merging deeply enough, you can view the past in such a way that you may actually see yourself in the past as some sort of apparition. Deep merges can often provide incredibly vivid details about places, events, and so forth. When your merging experience is not as deep, the images and sensations are mostly vague and fleeting.

The sensations you experience when merging range from relaxation, peacefulness, incredible calmness, and well-being to spinning, flying, whirling, and lightheadedness or heaviness. Often during merging, you find your awareness energetically floating as you feel yourself being both everything and nothing, at the same time. Death is the last Great Merge.

A few methods that can enhance your merging experience include using breathing exercises, staring at candlelight, making love, swimming, dancing, and chanting, as well as listening to special music, drumming, and visualization techniques. Liquor and psychoactive drugs can also induce merging. Other things that trigger merging experiences are exhaustion, near-death experiences, sudden injury, and illness.

The Circle

In Celtic custom, the man, representing the God, performs the preliminary rituals of "Drawing the Sacred Circle" and "Calling in the Four Watchtowers." The woman, representing the Great Goddess, hands him the elements of energy, and she is the one who performs the majority of the rituals. When you are working solitary, you perform both the roles of the Goddess and God.

The sacred circle is a protected space set up to do magic and ritual. It also serves as a vortex of light, which sets up a plane of communion between you and the Goddess and God. Most Celtic traditions cut a sacred circle to do any magical work and for all rituals. To cast the circle, visualize a bright blue-white flame shooting out of your outstretched hand (or the tip of your athame, or sword, or wand) as you spin in a clockwise circle. As you spin around, see and sense the area you want the circle to cover as ten feet in diameter, around the entire room, backyard, meadow clearing, and so forth.

Stand at the North point (where your altar is positioned), take the sprig of greenery, and dip it in the salt water (you can also use pinches of dry salt from the bowl). Wave the sprig gently in the North point, chanting out loud:

"Ayea, Ayea Kerridwen! Ayea, Ayea Kernunnos! Ayea, Ayea, Ayea!"

After purifying the North point, continue on to the East, South, and West points, respectively, sprinkling salt water at these corners and repeating the chant each time. When working with a partner or in a group, chant in unison if you like.

Next, face your altar and say:

"Blessed Be! Blessed Be the Gods! Blessed Be those who are gathered here."

You can add statements such as:

"I consecrate this circle of power to the ancient Goddesses and Gods. May they bless this circle with their presence and love."

Next merge with the Goddess and knock nine times on the surface of the altar with the handle of your wand, athame, knuckles, whatever, in three series of three. Your circle is now in place until you pull it up.

Calling in the Watchtowers

The Watchtowers are also called the Wards. They are ancient beings who protect and stand guard over your ritual circle. Each

Watchtower is ruled by a Watcher. The Watchers were originally the lesser gods, who watched over Earth and the celestial realms. They are the ancient Gods, sometimes referred to as the Ancient or Old Ones, who stand guard at the portals to the Otherworld(s).

Once you set your circle in place, you call the Watchtowers to stand guard at each of the four corners during ritual and magical work. Following is the procedure for doing this:

1. Place the tools with the elements in the center of your circle (most of the time this is on the altar). Take the bowl (or the high priestess hands it to the high priest) of salt or earth and stand at the North point. Sprinkle a bit of salt or earth on the ground.

2. Set the bowl down (or hand it back to the high priestess, who sets it down). Hold your athame in your right hand, and lift both of your arms, saying aloud,

   "Oh, great and mighty one, ruler of the North March, come, I pray you. Protect the gate of the North Ward. Come, I summon you!"

   Set down your athame if you are working solitary (either back on the altar or on a safe spot on the ground). If you are working with a partner, hand the athame to that person to hold.

3. Take the incense burner (lit) in your hands (or the high priestess hands it to you), and stand at the East point. Move the burner back and forth in front of you three times. Set the burner down or hand it back to your partner, and with your athame in your right hand, hold up your arms and say,

   "Oh, great and mighty one, ruler of the East March, come, I pray you. Protect the gate of the East Ward. Come, I summon you!"

   Set down your athame, or hand it back to your partner.

4. Take the candle holder with lit white candle (or your partner hands it to you), and stand at the South point. Wave the candle three times across the South point. Set the candle down carefully (or hand it back to your partner), and with your athame in your right hand, hold your arms upward and say,

> "Oh great and mighty one, ruler of the South March, come, I pray you. Protect the gate of the South Ward. Come, I summon you!"

> Set down your athame, or hand it back to the high priestess.

5. Take the chalice of water (or the high priestess hands it to you), and stand at the West point. Sprinkle nine drops (in three series of three) on the ground, and set the chalice down. Hold your athame in your right hand, and with your arms reaching upward, say,

> "Oh great and mighty one, ruler of the West March, come, I pray you. Protect the gate of the West Ward. Come, I summon you!"

> Set down your athame, or hand it back to the high priestess. The four Wards are now standing guard.

6. Move to the circle center and begin to chant the names of the Goddesses and Gods. Usually you chant.

> "Kerridwen, Kerridwen, Kerridwen, Kernunnos, Kernunnos, Kernunnos, Ayea, Ayea, Ayea!"

> You can also choose other Goddesses' and Gods' names to chant, particularly those deities you would like to help you in ritual.

7. Build and peak the power and energy and then direct it toward the work, ritual, or healing at hand. Swaying or dancing will build more power.

Cutting the Little Gate

After the four Wards are called into the circle, the man cuts a "Little Gate," which is usually an energetic gate located at the East point. He does this by holding his athame in his right hand, pointed outward, and starting at the bottom left edge of the door, moves his athame upward in a square or oval shape, ending at the bottom right point of the door, all the while seeing and sensing an energetic gate of blue-white light being created before him. The woman removes the four elements (the tools) from the circle. If you are working with a group, the others now enter the circle through the gate. The "Little Gate" is closed by reversing the process, the man handing the athame back to the woman, who places it back upon the altar.

Sample Celtic Wiccan Ritual

When working in a group, the customary greeting is,

"Merry meet and merry part; perfect love and perfect peace."
(Variation: Perfect love and perfect trust.)

Always make an effort to apply the Four Keys of Knowledge—self-honesty, self-responsibility, wisdom, and love—to every magical work you perform. You may also want to add background music and special lighting for your ritual. Intended for easy reference, the following is a 13-point checklist for rituals.

1. Define your purpose for doing the ritual or magical work.
2. Have a copy of the ritual on hand.
3. Gather your tools.
4. Set your altar.
5. Begin to move into a merged state of mind.
6. Open the circle.

7. Call the Watchtowers.
8. Invoke deities.
9. Do ritual.
10. Do healing Works.
11. Do magical works.
12. Toast the Goddesses and Gods (see page 203) and enjoy the feast (Variation: wine and cakes).
13. Pull up the circle.

Druid Healing Ritual for the Earth

Follow the steps numbered 1–10 in the previous 13-point ritual checklist. Then add the additional information that follows to fill in steps in the ritual checklist numbered 9–11. Finish up by following the instructions for steps numbered 12 and 13. Make certain you are clear about your intention and expectation in the healing ritual. Build your desire for a successful and powerful ritual, and make an effort to merge as deeply as you can with the Goddess and God.

Begin by standing facing the altar and saying out loud:

> "This is the time of all times.
> This is the place of all places.
> On this day the day of all days.
> I stand at the crossroads of worlds
> I stand before Goddess and God
> Lifting the veil of Mysteries.
> May the Shining Ones protect and guide me
> Blessed Be the Gods
> Blessed Be
> Blessed Be."

Take the bowl of salt (or earth) from the altar and hold it up toward the North point of your circle and say out loud:

"Great Mother Kerridwen, bless this bowl of salt unto your service. I call upon the powers of Earth to protect this circle and witness this rite."

Set the bowl back on the altar.

Take the burning incense from the altar and hold it up toward the east point of the circle and say,

"Great Father Kernunnos, bless this burning incense unto your service. I call upon the powers of Air to protect this circle and witness this rite."

Set the incense carefully back down upon the altar.

Take the candlestick and burning candle from the altar, and hold it up toward the South point of your circle and say,

"Great Father Kernunnos, bless this burning flame unto your service.

I call upon the powers of Fire to protect this circle and witness this rite."

Place the candle carefully back down on the altar.

Take the chalice of water from the altar and hold it upward toward the West point of the circle and say,

"Great Mother Kerridwen, bless this chalice of water unto your service. I call upon the powers of Water to protect this circle and witness this rite."

Place the chalice back down upon the altar.

Stand in the center of the circle and begin to loudly chant the names of the Goddesses and Gods you have selected to help you (see chapter 2). The Goddess and God names are customarily chanted three or nine times in succession, using alternating female and male deities. For example, if you chose Danu, Llyr, and Bridget, chant,

"Danu, Danu, Danu! Llyr, Llyr, Llyr! Bridget, Bridget, Bridget! Ayea, Ayea, Ayea!"

Do this several times.

Merge as deeply as you can, and see yourself holding a very young girl child. She is wounded and hurting, symbolizing the Earth as she is today. See yourself nurturing and comforting this child as you hold her, healing her with the light from your hands, heart, and head. Merge deeply with the divine energies and powers that be, and peak the energy, raising all of the power of the circle as you chant. If you so choose, raise the power in the form of a cone, with its tip toward the sky. Focus and allow the healing energy to flow through you and into the young girl in your arms, who symbolizes the Earth. Move the energy into her, healing her completely and watch as her wounds magically disappear as if they were never there. See and sense her smile at you, and return her smile with all of your being. When you are finished directing the healing energy, ground the power back to the circle and say three times,

"Blessed Be the Earth, may She ever thrive. Blessed Be the Mother, may She ever be reborn. Blessed Be the Gods."

To do any magical works, begin by saying out loud:

"The circle is bound
With power all around
In all worlds I stand
Protected in all lands."

Proceed with your magical works.
To bind your spells and works, say out loud:

"By the powers of the Goddess and God
by the sacred Earth, Moon, Stars, and Sun,

I bind the power within this circle
and ask that this work be done.
So mote it be
So be it.
Ayea, Ayea, Ayea!"

Take a few minutes to thank the Goddesses and Gods who have joined you in your sacred circle and helped you in your ritual and magical work. Say out loud,

"I wish you perfect love, and perfect peace. Blessed Be. Blessed Be. Blessed Be."

Toasting the Gods and Feasting

After the rituals on the Great Days and High Moons, it is the Celtic custom to toast the Goddesses and Gods. Participants fill their glasses with drink and select favorite Goddesses and Gods to toast to. For instance, you would raise your glass and say, "To Kerridwen, Ayea Great Lady. To Lugh, Ayea Master of all crafts."

Feasting is also traditional after the Great Day rituals. A special meal is prepared and eaten by all those who partake after the ritual. Feasting was one of the gifts the Dagda, the Good God, gave to humankind. The feast is a sacred meal in honor of the Goddess and God, and topics related to spirituality and magic are discussed by all those present in round table style.

Closing the Circle

At the end of the ritual, thank the Goddess and God once again for their rapport, kindness, and assistance. Also, it is time to allow the elemental energies to depart. Say out loud as you turn toward the appropriate directional point in the same pattern as you did previously,

"Oh powers of (element), depart in peace. Many blessings and thanks for your presence."

Pull up the sacred circle by using your athame. Holding your athame out in front of you, pointed outward, visualize the blue-white light of the circle being sucked into the blade. Move in a 360-degree counterclockwise circle when doing this procedure. Knock three times on the altar in honor of the Triple Goddess and God, and to release the Watchtowers. The ritual is now complete.

6

THE FUTURE OF CELTIC TRADITIONS

The past and future of Celtic traditions are being constantly related through the present. In this way, the profound concepts and philosophies that underpin Celtic mythology continue to greatly influence our conscious and unconscious minds. The mythic patterns within the ancient stories give us the keys to unlock the secrets of the magical Celtic traditions because it is through the stories that the magical images and archetypes are communicated and preserved.

The fascination with Celtic mythology and the power of the Celtic Goddesses and Gods has survived thousands of years, through onslaughts of war, pestilence, plague, religious persecution, and politicians, primarily because Celtic traditions are living traditions that are based on the concept of Oneness, where everything is connected to everything else and where everything, especially the land itself, is alive with energy and spirit, whether seen or unseen.

In Celtic traditions the sanctity of land and life are unified and harmonized together. The sacredness of the land is symbolized by the Goddess of Sovereignty, with all of us being her sons and daughters. This may indeed be the connection (DNA-based) between us all, as there were far less people in the past. There were fewer streams of lineage, and seeing as the Druids are known to have influenced, or have been influenced, by the peoples in Siberia, India, Egypt, Greece, most of the Mediterranean lands, and most of Europe, it is very possible that more of us may have Druid/Celtic roots and are more related to one another than we think. I propose that the "Druid Gene" may be actually be encoded deep within our DNA helix!

Whether genetic or not, because Celtic traditions are living traditions, the Celtic stories and deities are still very much alive in our hearts, minds, and spirits. This is reflected today as Celtic mythology and spirituality are being further revitalized and transformed by popular culture in forms such as this book, together with other publications, as well as works of music, films, television, the arts, fashion, and spiritual traditions such as Wicca and modern Druidism. In these ways, the divine power of the Celtic pantheon of Goddesses and Gods is as real and potent today as it was for our ancestors. This is likely to continue because their divine power is eternal and sleeping, existing in the very land itself, waiting to be awakened at times when they are most needed.

The Celts, and in particular the Druids, show us the importance of the power of place and where we find ourselves, reminding us to check in and connect with the land wherever we live. By attuning ourselves with the land and natural rhythms, we can tap into and create more harmony and unity within our lives. Nature is always speaking to us. We just need to remember to pay attention and listen for her signals and signs.

In this world torn by human hate, fanaticism, violence, and greed, there is much we can learn by opening our spirits up to the messages of nature: to the animals, trees, plants, stones, Sun, Moon, and Stars. By honoring the Great Mother and

Great Father, their magical, cosmic, and transcendent powers, and their rhythms, we can cultivate a reverence for the female and male forces in nature and come to a deeper understanding of those energies within ourselves and the human psyche. In the Druid tradition there is a saying: "To know deity is to know oneself, and to know oneself is to know deity." Now is the time to discover who and what you really are!

May your every breath, every act, every thought, and every dream be sacred.

May the veils between the worlds be lifted now and forevermore.

Blessed Be!

SOURCE DIRECTORY

All One Tribe Drum, (800) 442-DRUM, www.allonetribedrum.com
Handmade and hand-painted drums with Celtic symbols.

Amulets by Merlin, (804) 874-1476
Trees, forest spirits, and wizards, Celtic knotwork pieces in
filigree.

Ancient Circles, (800) 726-8032, www.pacific.net/- ancient
Fine Celtic jewelry, gold bermeil, sterling silver, torcs, moons,
knotwork, spirals.

Astral Seas, (800) 732-1734
Hand-crafted incense and oils, specialty items such as bath salts
and soaps. Custom Celtic or ancestral labeling and packaging
available.

Aureus, (800) 459-8463
Fine incense and oils.

Azure Green/Abyss Distribution, (413) 623-2155
Incense, scrying mirrors, candles, gifts, ritual items, cards, and
jewelry, books, tarot decks, talismans, and more.

Brigid's Fire, (800) 815-FIRE
Symbolic Celtic jewelry.

Central Casting, (800) 745-1350
Amulets, animal spirits, runestones, and sacred Goddesses.

Cheryl Briggs, (800) 548-5223
Celtic pendants, ritual chalices, wands, custom work.

Coyote Found Candles, (800) 788-4142.
Beeswax, plant vegetable, and standard candles. Source for

beeswax candles in the shape of the Goddess, beeswax kits, and prism candles in rainbow colors.

Crystal Courier Import, Inc., (800) 397-1863
Incense, wands, runes, crystals, and gemstones.

Damel Studio Ltd., (800) 89-DAMEL
Statuary and wall hangings of Celtic Goddesses and Fairies.

Deva Designs, (800) 799-8308
Goddess figurines, totem pendants.

Dryad Design, (800) 392-7705
Original designs by Paul Borda, Celtic statuary.

Earth Scents, (800) 933-5267
Oils, incense, aromatherapy.

Fellowship Foundry Pewtersmiths, (510) 352-0935
Pewter chalices, ritual tools, jewelry, handfasting cups, chalices, accessories, and statues.

Gabriele Masill Collection of Silver Jewelry, (800) 229-3731
Sterling silver jewelry with precious stones in the shapes of Celtic crosses, spirals, suns, and moons. Moonstone jewelry.

Heaven and Earth, (800) 942-9423
Metaphysical jewelry, gems, minerals, crystals, books.

Illusions by Design, (888) ILLUSION
Celtic knotwork, Celtic circles, spirals, and dragon T-shirts and sweats.

JBL Devotional Statues, (800) 290-6203, www.jblstatue.com/
Many Celtic Goddess and God statues.

Karen's Fine Art Products, (818) 798-9307
Celtic Goddess and fairy ornaments, cards, boxes, bookmarks, and decorative ceramic tiles.

Lost Mountain Trading Company, (800) 800-6319, lostmntn@coolstones.com
Runestones carved into semi-precious gemstones such as hematite, amethyst, citrine, and rose quartz, rune pendants, Celtic jewelry, Celtic rings for handfasting.

McNamara's Green, (206) 523-0306
Celtic stationery, notepads, Grail Quest cards, window decals,

T-shirts, bumper stickers, rubber stamps, jewelry, Celtic music, and books.

Mardigan's Maile: Chainmaile Catalog, (508) 759-1379
Exquisite chainmaile chaplets, handflowers, earrings, belts, bracelets, coifs, headbands, boot straps, chokers, bikini tops, and chainmaile shirts.

Mid-East Mfg., (407) 724-1477
Harps, bodhrans, bagpipes.

Nirvana Creations, (408) 384-0492
Greeting cards with visionary fantasy featuring Celtic Goddesses, fairies, and mermaids.

Open Circle Distributors, (800) 726-8032, ancient@pacific.net
Celtic jewelry, scarves, bags.

The Pendulum Works!, (800) 915-1151
Celtic-styled pendulums, crystal and gemstone pendulums, silk and cloth pouches.

Peter Stone, (410) 524-7400
Sterling, vermeil, and bermail jewelry. Rings, pendants, bracelets, and brooches. Celtic knotwork, original designs, and excellent craftsmanship.

Sacred Alchemy, (800) 522-0895
Pure essential ritual and healing oils with crystals.

Salem West, (614) 421-7557, www.neopagan.com
One of the most complete Celtic supply stores, with ritual kits, oils, an extensive selection of books, herbs, jewelry, statues, masks, incense and burners, drums, crystals, gemstones, custom-made ritual tools, and ceramics.

Shabda, (800) 678-3013
Incense, amber charms, candles, Celtic jewelry.

Sign of the Harp, (617) 749-8784
Jewelry from hand-sculpted original designs.

Sorcerer's Apprentice, (608) 271-7591
Silk robes, altar cloths, incense, and gemstones.

Sun's Eye, (800) SUNS EYE (786-7393)
Mystical oil, bath salts, candles, hand-blended formulary oils.

Visabella, (800) 474-9567
  Velvet ritual gowns and hooded capes.

Waterhawk Creations, (216) 666-8745
  Boxes, pendants, ritual tools, one-of-a-kind pieces.

The Wax House, (888) WAX-9711, www.waxhouse.com
  Candlemaking supplies, beeswax sheets in every color of the
  rainbow, molds, and candle oils.

Wellstone, (800) 544-8773
  Fine jewelry in sterling silver or 14K gold, symbols of the Green
  Man, Herne, spirals, torcs, and moons available. Images with and
  without gemstones.

Whispered Prayers, (530) 894-2927, www.whisperedprayers.com
  Incense, smudge, altar tiles, jewelry, candles, ritual tools, oils,
  herbs, scrying mirrors, robes, books, crystals, and gemstones.

WindRose Trading Co., Inc., (800) 229-3731
  Incense, incense holders, rolled Tibetan incense, diffusers, stone
  statues, perfume oils, hand-painted rainbow silk bags.

Winds of Tyme, (604) 987-0767
  Celtic giftware, greeting cards, bookmarks, key chains, art prints,
  Celtic Cross replicas, pewterware, and jewelry.

Windstone Editions, (800) 982-4464
  Beautiful forest wizard statues and the like.

Z Productions, (972) 438-2072
  Robes, capes with Celtic trim, ritual tools and cloths, many with
  Celtic designs.

Recommended Additions to Your Celtic / Wiccan Library

Advanced Wicca by Patricia Telesco
Anam Cara by John O'Donohue
The Art of Celtia by Courtney Davis
Born in Albion: The Re-Birth of the Craft by David Williams
and Kate West
Celebrating the Great Mother by Cait Johnson and Maura Shaw
Celtic Bards, Celtic Druids by R. J. Stewart and Robin Williamson
The Celtic Book of Days by Caitlin Matthews
The Celtic Druids' Year by John King
Celtic Gods, Celtic Goddesses by R. J. Stewart
The Celtic Lunar Zodiac by Helena Paterson
Celtic Mandalas by Courtney Davis, text by Helena Paterson
Celtic Myths, Celtic Legends by R. J. Stewart
Celtic Tarot by Courtney Davis and Helena Paterson
Celtic Women in Legend, Myth and History by Lyn Webster
Wilde Co.
The Celts by Jean Markale
Cerridwen's Handbook of Incense, Oils, and Candles by Maya Heath
Circle Round: Raising Children in Goddess Traditions by Starhawk,
Diane Baker, and Anne Hill
Drawing Down the Moon by Margot Alder
Dreampower Tarot by R. J. Stewart
The Druids by Peter B. Ellis
A Druid's Herbal for the Sacred Earth Year by Ellen Hopman
Earth Magic: A Dianic Book of Shadows by Marion Weinstein
Earthlight by R. J. Stewart

Everyday Magic by Dorothy Morrison
Fairy & Folk Tales of Ireland, edited by W. B. Yeats
Greenfire: Making Love With the Goddess by Sirona Knight
Handbook of Celtic Astrology by Helena Paterson
History of the Kings of Britain by Geoffrey Monmouth
Isle of Avalon by Nicholas Mann
King Arthur and the Grail Quest by John Matthews
King Arthur's Return by Courtney Davis, text by Helena Paterson
King of the Celts by Jean Markale
Legend: The Arthurian Tarot by Anna-Marie Ferguson
Living Wicca by Scott Cunningham
The Living World of Faery by R. J. Stewart
Love, Sex, and Magick by Sirona Knight
The Mabinogi by Patrick Ford
Merlin, Priest of Nature by Jean Markale
Merlin Tarot by R. J. Stewart
Moonflower: Erotic Dreaming With the Goddess by Sirona Knight
Notions and Potions by Susan Bowes
The Pocket Guide to Celtic Spirituality by Sirona Knight
The Pocket Guide to Wicca by Paul Tuitean and Estelle Daniels
Positive Magic by Marion Weinstein
The Power Within the Land by R. J. Stewart
The Seasons of the Sun by Patricia Telesco
Secret Tradition in Arthurian Legend by Gareth Knight
Secrets of Ancient and Sacred Places by Paul Devereux
The Shapeshifter Tarot by Sirona Knight and D. J. Conway
Spinning Spells, Weaving Wonders by Patricia Telesco
Spiral Dance by Starhawk
The Stones of Time by Martin Brennan
21st Century Wicca by Jennifer Hunter
The Unknown Arthur by John Matthews
What Witches Do by Stuart Farrar
The White Goddess by Robert Graves
Wicca for Men by A. J. Drew
Wiccan Mysteries by Raven Grimassi
Wisdom of the Elements by Margie McArthur
Witch in Every Woman by Laurie Cabot, with Jean Mills
A Witches Bible: The Complete Witches' Handbook by Janet
   and Stewart Farrar
Women of the Celts by Jean Markale

Favorite Celtic Music Titles

Alan Stivell in Concert
At the End of the Evening by Nightnoise
Banba by Clannad
Celtic Christmas II by various artists
Celtic Cross by Richard Searles
Celtic Crossroads by John Whelan and Friends.
A Celtic Evening with Derek Bell, featuring Maireid Sullivan
Celtic Forest by various artists
Celtic Harp 1, 2, 3, and 4 by Patrick Ball
Celtic Heart: The Story of Tristan and Iseult by Simon Cooper
Celtic Heartbeat Christmas by various artists
Celtic Soul by Noirin Ni Riain
Celtic Spirit by various artists
Celtic Tale by Mychael and Jeff Danna
Celtic Treasure: The Legacy of Turlough O'Carolan by various artists
Celtic Twilight by various artists
Celtic Twilight Two by various artists
Celtic Twilight Three: Lullabies by various artists
The Celts by Enya
Circle of the Sun by Aine Minogue
Dancer by Maireid Sullivan
Druid by Medwyn Goodall
Elemental by Loreena McKennitt
Emerald Castles by Richard Searles
Excalibur by Medwyn Goodall
Fairy of the Woods by Gary Stadler
Gothic Dream by Pilgrim

Legende by Alan Stivell
The Long Black Veil by the Chieftans
Lore by Clannad
Love's Caress by Maireid Sullivan
The Mask and Mirror by Loreena McKennitt
The Memory of Trees by Enya
Merlin by Medwyn Goodall
Misty Eyed Adventures by Maire Brennan
The Mystic Harp by Derek Bell
Myth & Magic by various artists
Parting Tide by Nightnoise
Renaissance of the Celtic Harp by Alan Stivell
Riverdance by Bill Whelan (also available on video)
Santiago by the Chieftans
Scottish Christmas by Maggie Sansone
Shepherd Moons by Enya
Sons of Somerled by Steve McDonald
Tir Nan Og by Alan Stivell
The Visit by Loreena McKennitt
Watermark by Enya
Women of the World: Celtic by various artists
Wood, Fire, and Gold by Kim Robertson

Bibliography

Anderson, Rosemarie. *Celtic Oracles.* New York: Harmony Books, 1998.

Baumgartner, Anne. *A Comprehensive Dictionary of the Gods.* New York: University Books, 1984.

Blair, Nancy. *Amulets of the Goddess.* Oakland, California: Wingbow Press, 1993.

Bolen, Jean Shinoda, M.D. *Goddessess in Every Woman.* New York: Harper & Row, 1984.

Bonwick, James. *Irish Druids and Old Irish Religions.* New York: Dorset, 1986.

Bord, Janet, and Colin Bord. *Mysterious Britain.* London: Paladin Books, 1974.

Bowes, Susan. *Notions and Potions.* New York: Sterling Publishing Co., Inc., 1997.

Briggs, K. M. *The Fairies in English Tradition and Literature.* Chicago: University of Chicago Press, 1967.

Bromwich, Rachael. *The Welsh Triads.* Cardiff: University of Wales Press, 1961.

Bulfinch, Thomas. *Bulfinch's Mythology.* Garden City, New York: Garden City Publishing Co., Inc., 1938.

Campbell, Joseph. *The Power of Myth.* New York: Doubleday, 1988.

_____. *Transformation of Myth Through Time.* New York: Harper & Row, 1990.

_____. *The Masks of God, Vols I–IV.* New York: Penguin Books, 1977.

Carr-Gomm, Philip. *The Druid Way.* Rockport, Massachusetts: Element Books, Inc., 1993.

Ceram, C. W. *Gods, Graves and Scholars.* New York: Bantam Books, 1972.

Drew, A. J. *Wiccan for Men.* Secaucus, New Jersey: Citadel Press, 1998.

Eliade, Mircea. *Shamanism*. Princeton, New Jersey: Bollingen Series, 1964.

Ellis, Peter Berresford. *The Druids*. Grand Rapids, Michigan: William B. Eerdmans Publishing Company, 1994.

Evans-Wentz, W. Y. *The Fairy Faith in Celtic Countries*. New York: Citadel Press, 1990.

Farrar, Janet and Stewart. *The Witches' Way*. London: Robert Hale, 1984.

Farrar, Stewart. *What Witches Do*. London: Peter Davis Limited, 1971.

Ford, Patrick K., translator. *The Mabinogi and Other Medieval Welsh Tales*. Los Angeles: University of California Press, 1977.

Frazier, Sir James George. *The Golden Bough*. New York: The Macmillan Company, 1935.

Gaster, Theodor, editor. *The New Golden Bough*. New York: The New American Library, 1959.

Gimbutas, Marija. *The Goddesses and Gods of Old Europe*. Berkeley, California: University of California Press, 1982.

_____. *The Language of the Goddess*. San Francisco: Harper & Row, 1989.

Glass, Justine. *They Foresaw the Future*. New York: G. P. Putnam's Sons, 1969.

Gramsi, Raven. *The Wiccan Mysteries*. St. Paul, Minnesota: Llewellyn Publications, 1997.

Graves, Robert. *The White Goddess*. New York: Faber & Faber, 1966.

Grimal, Pierre, editor. *Larousse World Mythology*. London: Paul Hamlyn, 1965.

Heath, Maya. *Cerridwen's Handbook of Incense, Oils, and Candles*. San Antonio, Texas: Words of Wizdom International, Inc., 1996.

Jung, Carl G.. *The Archetypes of the Collective Unconscious*. Princeton, New Jersey: Princeton University Press, 1990.

King, John. *The Celtic Druids' Year*. London: Blandford, 1994.

Knight, Gareth. *The Secret Tradition in Arthurian Legend*. York Beach, Maine: Samuel Weiser, Inc., 1996.

Knight, Sirona. *Greenfire: Making Love with the Goddess*. St. Paul, Minnesota: Llewellyn Publications, 1995.

_____. *Love, Sex, and Magick*. Secaucus, New Jersey: Carol Publishing Group, 1999.

_____. *Moonflower: Erotic Dreaming With the Goddess*. St. Paul, Minnesota: Llewellyn Publications, 1996.

_____. *The Pocket Guide to Celtic Spirituality*. Freedom, California: Crossing Press, 1998.

_____. *The Pocket Guide to Crystals and Gemstones*. Freedom, California: Crossing Press, 1998.

Knight, Sirona, et al. *The Shapeshifter Tarot*. St. Paul, Minnesota: Llewellyn Publications, 1998.

Leach, Maria, editor. *Standard Dictionary of Folklore, Mythology, and Legend*. New York: Funk & Wagnalls Co., 1950.

Markale, Jean. *The Celts*. Rochester, Vermont: Inner Traditions International, 1993.

_____. *Merlin: Priest of Nature*. Rochester, Vermont: Inner Traditions, 1995.

_____. *Women of the Celts*. Rochester, Vermont: Inner Traditions, 1986.

Matthews, John. *Taliesin: Shamanic and Bardic Mysteries in Britain and Ireland*. London: Aquarian Press, 1988.

Monaghan, Patricia. *The Book of Goddesses and Heroines*. St. Paul, Minnesota: Llewellyn Publications, 1990.

Mormouth, Geoffrey. *History of the Kings of Britain*. New York: E. P. Dutton & Co., 1958.

Morris, Jan. *A Matter of Wales*. Oxford: Oxford University Press, 1984.

Murray, Margaret. *The God of the Witches*. London: Oxford University Press, 1970.

O'Donohue, John. *Anam Cara: A Book of Celtic Wisdom*. New York: HarperCollins, 1997.

Paterson, Helena. *Handbook of Celtic Astrology*. St. Paul, Minnesota: Llewellyn Publications, 1995.

Piggott, Stuart. *The Druids*. London: Thames & Hudson, 1976.

Rees, Alwyn and Brinley. *Celtic Heritage, Ancient Tradition in Ireland and Wales*. New York: Grove Press, 1978.

Ross, Anne. *Pagan Celtic Britain*. New York: Columbia University Press, 1967.

Sitchin, Zecharia. *When Time Began*. Santa Fe, New Mexico: Bear and Company, 1993.

Smith, Sir William. *Smaller Classical Dictionary*. New York: E. P. Dutton, 1958.

Spence, Lewis. *The History and Origins of Druidism*. New York: Samuel Weiser, Inc., 1971.

Stewart, R. J. *The Power Within the Land*. Rockport, Maine: Element Books, 1992.

_____. *Celtic Gods, Celtic Goddesses.* New York: Sterling Publishing Co., 1990.

_____. *Earth Light.* Rockport, Maine: Element Books, 1992.

_____. *The Living World of Faery.* Glastonbury, Somerset: Gothic Image Publication, 1995.

Stewart, R. J. and Robin Williamson. *Celtic Druids, Celtic Bards.* London: Blandford Press, 1996.

Telesco, Patricia. *The Herbal Arts.* Secaucus, New Jersey: Citadel Press, 1998.

Valiente, Doreen. *The Rebirth of Witchcraft.* London: Robert Hale, 1989.

_____. *Witchcraft for Tomorrow.* New York: St. Martin's Press, 1978.

Wilde, Lady. *Ancient Legends, Mystic Charms and Superstitions of Ireland.* New York: Lemma Publishing, 1973.

Williams, David and Kate West. *Born in Albion: The Re-Birth of the Craft.* Runcorn, U. K.: Pagan Media Ltd., 1996.

Worwood, Valerie. *The Complete Book of Essential Oils and Aromatherapy.* New York: New World Library, 1995.

Yeats, W. B., editor. *Fairy & Folk Tales of Ireland.* New York: Macmillan Publishing Co., 1983.

INDEX

About the Author

Practicing the craft for over fourteen years, SIRONA KNIGHT is a High Priestess and Third Degree Craft Master of the California Gwyddonic Druid Tradition. She is the author of several books on Celtic traditions and Wicca, including *Love, Sex, and Magick*; *The Pocket Guide to Celtic Spirituality*; *Greenfire: Making Love With the Goddess*; and *Moonflower: Erotic Dreaming With the Goddess*. In addition, Sirona is the author of the popular *Shapeshifter Tarot* deck, which is based on Celtic shamanism.

Sirona is a contributing editor for *Magical Blend* magazine, and is also a contributing writer for *New Age Retailer* and *Aquarius* magazines. She has a master's degree in psychology and is a hypnotherapist. She makes frequent media appearances, on both radio and television, and maintains a Web page at www.dcsi.net/~bluesky, answers e-mail (bluesky@dcsi.net) from fans, and chats regularly on pagan Web sites across the country. Sirona also lectures and teaches workshops across the United States and has a Druid college (The College of the Sun), where she trains students in Druid spirituality and practices.

Sirona lives in the woods of northern California (Goddess Country!) with her family; Michael, her husband and spiritual partner, and Skylor, their son, four beagles, and a family of cats. She is a vegetarian, avid animal lover, outspoken tree-hugger, and star gazer. Her interests include interviewing interesting people, reading everything she can get her hands on, homeschooling, singing, writing poetry, surfing the Internet, collecting and working with crystals and stones, as well as divination, eating popcorn and watching classic movies, and tending her rose and vegetable gardens.